P9-EES-089

A TASTE of the ARTS

edited by: Patricia Schlosser

published by
the Edmonton Arts Cookbook Society
as a unique joint fundraising venture
of the following organizations:

ALBERTA BALLET GUILD, EDMONTON CHAPTER
AURORA SOCIETY OF NORTHERN LIGHT THEATRE
EDMONTON OPERA GUILD
JUBILEE OPERA GUILD
WOMEN'S COMMITTEE OF THE
EDMONTON SYMPHONY SOCIETY
WOMEN'S SOCIETY OF THE
EDMONTON ART GALLERY

All proceeds from the sale of this book will be used to support the
cultural activities of these organizations.

A TASTE
of the
ARTS

Printed by Centax of Canada
Regina, Saskatchewan

Photography by Con Boland,
Middle Earth Gallery
Edmonton, Alberta

copyright © 1982
Edmonton Arts Cookbook Society
P.O. Box 9528
Edmonton, Alberta
Canada   T6E 5X2

all rights reserved

First printing — September 1982 . . . 10,000 books

Canadian Cataloguing in Publication Data

A Taste of the arts

Includes index.
ISBN 0-9691185-0-3

1. Cookery. I. Schlosser, Patricia. 2. Edmonton
Arts Cookbook Society

TX715.T37   641.5   C82-090130-X

DEDICATION

This book is dedicated to all of the volunteers who have over many years, initiated and sustained with flair, enthusiasm and endless hard work the various societies and organizations committed to the advancement of the arts and culture in the communities in which they live. They have greatly enriched our lives.

FUNDING FOR THIS BOOK HAS BEEN PROVIDED BY:

Mr. & Mrs. John L. Schlosser
Mrs. W. H. Schlosser
Dr. & Mrs. J. D. M. Alton
Mr. & Mrs. C. Thomas Peacocke
Alberta Ballet Guild, Edmonton Chapter
Aurora Society of Northern Light Theatre
Edmonton Opera Guild
Jubilee Opera Guild
Women's Committee of the Edmonton Symphony Society
Women's Society of the Edmonton Art Gallery
Alberta Culture

Legal guidance has been provided by Matheson and Company.

When six organizations get together to sponsor a project such as this — THINGS GET DONE! From organizers and planners, to testers, typers, manuscript readers, art and photography designers, promoters, distributors and all of the other helpers, the enthusiastic and energetic support has been gratifying. Thank you

Elinor Mix	Doreen Mason
Barbara McLeod	Betty Jean Buchanan
Irma Young	Alta Wood
Maureen Hemingway	Marion Ramsay
Bobbie Patrick	Helen Schlosser
Catie Allan	Irma Marchiel
Eleanor Clark	Barbara Allan
Lorraine Gillespie	Paddy Fernandez-Davila
Vicki Vaitkunus	Judy Ross
Kathie Leitch	Mary Lansky
Janet Bentley	Phyllis Borehem
Judy Peacocke	Carole Lavalee
Nancy Lieberman	Mrs. H. Justus
Gratzia Poretti	Dana Green-Laing
Mary Maclean	F. Phillips
Chris Backhaus	R. Martens
Elizabeth Hyde	Isabel Smith
Helen Potter	E. Johnson
Bill Slavik	Maria Covassi
Jane Alton	Gertrude Burch
Liz Brandt	Don Delaney
Helen Hope	Joan Manuel
Audrey Martyn	Gwen Watters
George Botchett	Jan Quigley
Rob Hood	Ruby Swekla
Jane Sturgeon	Connie Ursino
Barbara Hunt	Mary Pardee
Dodie Sherbaniuk	Jean Cooper
Berenice Dunsworth	Maria Loterzo
Maryalice Kennedy	Pauline Nay
Joyce Harries	Joyce Hawkes
Jeanne Johnston	Peggy Matheson
Sydney Turner	Joan Dickins
Audrey Bishop	Claire Kirkland
Marion Shipley	Ruth Mansfield
Elizabeth Welsh	Elexis Schloss
Marnie Sproule	Joan Hawkins
Lynn Winter	Barbara Horowitz

FOREWORD —

Here is a collection of recipes from people who love to cook. Many are practical, a few are whimsical, some demand total dedication and some, considerable time. They are all tried and true favorites. One, I know is based on a recipe more than 100 years old. THAT is really an HEIRLOOM!

We have worked on this book for over a year. In that time, hundreds of recipes have been collected and each has been carefully tested.

We hope you will find helpful our recipes for feeding 24 — be it a party for the school team or the visiting guest artist. For an easy celebration on a Wednesday night — that's Midweek Gourmet. A picnic by the trout pond? Look up Déjeuner sur l'Herbe. Something soul satisfying that your Grandmother used to bake — see Heirlooms. Planning to have the neighbors in for coffee — open up the chapter on Tea, Coffee and Cocktails. And because we just had to include some more — see ENCORE!

And so — to you who enjoy cooking and sharing recipes — Here is our book. We hope that many of these recipes will become your favorites.

Patricia Schlosser
Editor

Cover picture:
Chicken Kaleidoscope

CONTENTS

Twenty-Four or More

Top picture: Avocado Crepes

Bottom picture: (from the top in
                    clockwise direction)
                    Candied Almonds
                    Swedish Almond Cream
                       with Strawberries
                    Daiquiri Soufflé

These recipes are for 24 or more servings. Make more for second servings.

Twenty-Four or More

Top picture: Avocado Crepes

Bottom picture: (from the top in
clockwise direction)
Candied Almonds
Swedish Almond Cream
  with Strawberries
Daiquiri Soufflé

These recipes are for 24 or more servings. Make more for second servings.

Top picture: Avocado Crepes

Bottom picture: (from the top in
                    clockwise direction)
                    Candied Almonds
                    Swedish Almond Cream
                      with Strawberries
                    Daiquiri Soufflé

These recipes are for 24 or more servings. Make more for second servings.

Twenty-Four or More

CHILLED AVOCADO SOUP 1

Serves 24

6 cups rich chicken broth
6 avocados, peeled and chopped
1/2 cup dry sherry
1 teaspoon salt
1 teaspoon minced onion
1/2 teaspoon dill weed
2 1/2 cups light cream

In a blender or food processor, in convenient amounts, whirl avocado, sherry, salt, onion and dill weed, with some of the broth, until smooth. Put the puree into a large pitcher or urn, adding remaining broth and cream. Stir, cover tightly and chill until ready to serve.

CREAM OF BROCCOLI SOUP 2

Serves 24

2 cups minced onion
1 cup thinly sliced celery
1 cup thinly sliced leeks
1 clove garlic, finely minced
1/4 cup butter
3 pounds broccoli cut in 1-inch pieces
12 cups chicken stock
4 cups light cream
salt
pepper

Wash broccoli and trim into flowerettes and tender stalks. Peel stalks to remove any tough outer layer.

In a large pan sweat the onion, celery, leeks and garlic in the butter, covered over low heat for 20 minutes.

Add the chicken stock and peeled stalks of broccoli and simmer 15 minutes.

Add flowerettes and simmer 15 minutes more.

Puree the mixture in a blender or food processor and stir in the cream.

Add the salt and pepper to taste.

Serve piping hot, garnished with parsley.

3   ZUCCHINI SALAD

Serves 24

10 zucchini, long and thin, sliced, skins on
1 green pepper, chopped
1/4 cup chopped green onion
1/4 cup chopped parsley

1 package Italian salad dressing mix
1 cup salad oil
1/4 cup vinegar
1/2 cup pickle relish
1/2 cup sauterne

Combine zucchini, pepper, onion and parsley in large bowl.

Combine dressing ingredients — Italian mix, oil, vinegar, relish, sauterne. Add to vegetables and marinate overnight.

4   SCHNIPPLED BEAN SALAD

*Serves
24-30*

4 pounds frozen French-cut green beans
3 onions (about 2 1/2 inches in diameter)
salt
pepper

Cook beans briefly so that they are tendercrisp and retain their bright green colour. Quickly rinse in cold water and drain immediately. Meanwhile, peel and slice onions — place in a bowl and sprinkle liberally with salt. (3-4 Tablespoons). Let stand at least 1/2 hour, stirring occasionally. Onions should be limp. Squeeze onion rings between palms of your hands (wear rubber gloves!) to remove as much juice as possible. Do not rinse. Mix onions and beans with sour cream dressing. Chill well. This can be made a day ahead. Stir well before serving.

Sour Cream Dressing:
4 teaspoons vinegar
4 teaspoons sugar
1-2 teaspoons salt
3 cups sour cream

Blend well.

BISHOP'S SALAD 5

Serves 24

3 packages frozen artichoke hearts
1 package Italian salad dressing mix
3 cups thinly sliced mushrooms
3 3-ounce packages lemon gelatine
5 1/4 cups boiling water
1 small jar chopped pimento, drained
1 cup mayonnaise

Prepare artichokes as directed on package. Cut pieces in half. Put in bowl with sliced mushrooms.

Prepare salad dressing mix as directed. Pour over artichokes and mushrooms, and marinate one hour. Drain; reserve dressing.

Prepare the gelatine, using 5 1/4 cups water. Refrigerate until consistency of unbeaten egg white.

Fold in artichoke mixture and pimento.

Pour into large mold. Refrigerate until firm.

Serve, unmolded and garnished, with a dressing of mayonnaise combined with the reserved marinade.

MARINATED ONIONS, WITH SOUR CREAM 6

Serves 24

2-4 Spanish onions
1/2 cup white vinegar
1/2 cup water
2 Tablespoons brown sugar
1 1/2 cups sour cream
1/2 teaspoon caraway seeds or celery seed

Soak thinly sliced onions in vinegar, water and brown sugar for at least 4 hours.

Drain. Add sour cream and caraway seeds or celery seeds.

Keeps well.

7   GOOD LADY CHICKEN SALAD

Serves 24

18 pounds chicken, bone included
2 2/3 cups mayonnaise
1 cup light cream
1/2 cup vinegar
3 Tablespoons grated onion
1/2 teaspoon white pepper
5 teaspoons salt
7 cups seeded, halved green grapes
4 cups thinly sliced celery
2 cups slivered almonds, toasted
3 large heads lettuce

Day before serving, prepare chicken. Oven-poach broiler/fryers about 45 minutes or simmer stewing chicken 3 to 4 hours, reserving broth for another day. Cool and remove meat from skin and bones, then cut into chunks. Refrigerate.

About 3 hours before serving, combine the dressing ingredients: mayonnaise, cream, vinegar, onion, pepper and salt. Combine chicken, grapes, celery and almonds. Add dressing, toss gently. Cover and refrigerate.

At serving time heap 1 cup of salad onto individual lettuce leaves on plates.

8   GRAPEFRUIT CUCUMBER MOLD

Serves 24

2 — 6 ounce packages lime Jello
1 teaspoon salt
4 cups boiling water
2 — 15 ounce cans sweetened grapefruit
    sections with the syrup
3 cups cucumber, coarsely grated and
    well drained
2 cups chopped celery
greens, and unpeeled cucumber slices for
    garnish

Dissolve gelatine and salt in hot water.

Add grapefruit sections with syrup. Cool until mixture begins to thicken.

Stir in cucumber and celery. Pour into molds or shallow pans. Chill until firm.

Unmold, or cut into squares and serve on a bed of crisp greens, garnished with cucumber slices.

Serves 24

5 cups creamed cottage cheese
2 — 8 ounce packages cream cheese
3 Tablespoons gelatin
3/4 cup cold water
1 teaspoon salt
5-6 cups green grapes
1 cup broken pecans
1/4 cup chopped chives
3 cups whipping cream, whipped

Blend the cheeses.

Soften the gelatine in cold water, then dissolve over boiling water. Add salt. Stir into cheese mixture.

Add grapes, nuts and chives, fold in the whipped cream.

Pour into large oiled mold. Chill 4 to 6 hours (or overnight).

Unmold on lettuce lined platter.

Serve with honey or lemonade dressing.

Honey Dressing for Fruit Cheese Mold:
1/2 cup sugar
1 teaspoon dry mustard
1 teaspoon paprika
1 teaspoon celery seed
1/4 teaspoon salt
1/3 cup liquid honey
1 teaspoon grated onion
1/3 cup vinegar
1 Tablespoon lemon juice
1 cup salad oil

Combine all ingredients, adding oil at the last, beating constantly. Makes about 2 cups.

Lemonade Dressing:
2 eggs
1/2 cup sugar
1 — 6 ounce can frozen lemonade concentrate, undiluted
1 cup whipping cream, whipped

Beat eggs in top of double boiler. Stir in sugar and lemonade. Cook and stir over boiling water until thick. Cool, and fold in the whipped cream. Makes 3 cups.

10 DEE'S TOMATO PUDDING

Serves 24

3 large cans tomatoes
6 small cans tomato Puree
3 cups brown sugar
3/4 cup butter
6 cups fresh cubed bread
salt and pepper to taste

In a well buttered casserole, mix all ingredients.

Bake slowly (325ºF-350ºF) for 1 1/2 to 2 hours, until bubbly and brown.

May be cooked the day before and re-heated before serving.

11 SWEET AND SOUR COLESLAW

Serves 24

3 pounds grated or shredded green cabbage
3 green peppers, shredded
2 onions, chopped fine

Sprinkle 2 cups sugar over vegetables and let stand in china bowl.

1 cup salad oil
1 teaspoon salt
1 cup vinegar
2 teaspoons sugar
2 teaspoons celery seed

Mix in saucepan and bring to boil. Boil 3 minutes, stirring well. Immediately pour over vegetables. Let stand covered tightly, several hours before using. Will keep in refrigerator for 9 days.

VEGETABLES AU GRATIN

Serves 24

broccoli or cauliflower flowerettes
6 Tablespoons butter
6 Tablespoons flour
1 teaspoon salt
3 cups milk
3 cups grated, *sharp* Cheddar cheese
1 1/2 teaspoons Beau Monde
2 teaspoons grated lemon peel
1/3 cup chopped pecans, if desired

Melt butter in saucepan. Add flour and salt. Cook gently for 2 minutes. Remove from heat and briskly stir in milk. Return to heat and cook, stirring constantly until smooth and thickened, and raw flour taste has disappeared. Add 2 cups of grated cheese. Stir to melt cheese, then add the Beau Monde and lemon peel. Drop vegetables into boiling, salted water and cook briefly. Drain while still slightly crisp. Place vegetables in large, broad baking dish and cover with cheese sauce. Sprinkle with remaining 1 cup cheese and pecans.

This may be covered and refrigerated until dinner, at which time bake, covered with foil, for 30 minutes at 350ºF; uncover and continue to bake until cheese bubbles and browns.

ARTICHOKE CHEESE SQUARES

Serves 24

3 Tablespoons bacon dripping or oil
1 cup chopped green onion
3 garlic cloves, mashed
12 eggs beaten to frothy
6 cans (14 ounces each) artichokes, drained
3/4 cup dry bread crumbs
1 pound Swiss or Cheddar cheese, shredded
1/4 cup minced parsley

Cook onion and garlic in bacon drippings or oil until tender. Combine all the ingredients, withholding 1/4 cup bread crumbs for topping. Spread out in 2 large (9" x 13") greased pans. Sprinkle with remaining crumbs. Bake at 325ºF for 30 minutes. Allow to "set" a few minutes before serving.

May be refrigerated and re-heated.

14 TOMATOES STUFFED WITH SPINACH

Serves 24

24 medium, or 12 large tomatoes
12 slices bacon, diced
2 packages of frozen, chopped spinach
1 1/2 cups soft bread crumbs
    (whirl fresh bread in a blender or
    food processor)
1/2 teaspoon pepper
salt

Cut tops off tomatoes (or cut large tomatoes in half). Partially scoop out centers, using the pulp for other cooking. Turn upside down to drain. Cook bacon until crisp and drain. Cook and drain spinach.

Combine spinach, crumbs, bacon, salt and pepper. Spoon the mixture into the salted tomatoes and arrange in a greased baking pan. The tomatoes and the spinach mixture can be prepared early in the day, and refrigerated.

Bring to room temperature.

Bake uncovered in 350ºF oven for 20 minutes.

Tomatoes should be tender, and very hot, but should hold their shape.

15 CHEESY-POTATO CASSEROLE

*Serves
20-24*

6 pounds potatoes, peeled
1 cup butter
1 cup cream cheese
1 teaspoon salt
2 green peppers, chopped
2 bunches green onions, chopped
1 cup Cheddar cheese, grated
1 cup Parmesan cheese, grated
1/2 teaspoon saffron
1 small tin pimento, minced, plus juice

Boil and mash the potatoes, adding butter, cream cheese and salt. Then add remaining ingredients, whipping constantly. Mixture will be fairly moist. Turn into a large, open baking dish. Bake at 350ºF for 30 minutes.

CHEESE AND ONION PIE

Serves 24

3 unbaked pie shells
9 large onions, thinly sliced
1/2 cup butter
4 cups milk
9 eggs
salt
pepper
6 cups mild grated cheese

Saute onions in butter in a large skillet until tender, but not brown. Divide into 3 — 9" pans lined with chilled pastry. Sprinkle with grated cheese. Scald milk, blend in the beaten eggs, salt and pepper, and pour over the cheese-covered onions.

Bake at 350ºF for 40 minutes, until filling is set.

NEVER FAIL RICH PASTRY,
FOR QUICHES AND PIES

Serves 24

5 cups flour
1 teaspoon baking powder
1 teaspoon salt
1 Tablespoon sugar
1 pound lard at room temperature
1 egg
water
1 Tablespoon vinegar

Sift flour, baking powder, salt and pepper. Bring lard to room temperature and cut into dry ingredients.

Put egg in measuring cup. Fill to 3/4 cup mark with water and add vinegar. Stir this mixture into flour-lard mixture until moistened. Knead about 8 times gently. Roll out.

Freeze shells unbaked, ready for filling.

Note: Sugar may be omitted for main course pastry cases.

18   BEEF AND OYSTER PIE

Serves 24

Uncooked pastry, enough to cover 2 large
    baking dishes
8 pounds sirloin or roundsteak, cubed
4 cups chopped onion
6 cups consomme (almost 5 cans)
1 small can tomato paste
2 Tablespoons sugar
2 Tablespoons Worcestershire sauce
2 cups red wine
8 cans oysters, drained

Coat the cubed steak in mixture of flour, salt and pepper, and brown in a small amount of oil or bacon fat. Add remaining ingredients — onion, consomme, tomato paste, sugar, Worcestershire sauce, wine and oysters. Place mixture in 2 medium flat baking dishes. Cover with pastry. Bake at 350°F approximately 1 hour.

19   WILD RICE CURRY

Serves 24

2 cups wild rice
4 cups brown rice
15 slices bacon, diced
3 cups chopped onion
3 cups sliced mushrooms
3 cups raw, grated carrot
6 eggs
3 cups whole milk
3 Tablespoons curry powder
1 Tablespoon salt
1/2 cup butter

Cook rice until well done. Drain.

Fry bacon until crisp, draining off most of the fat. Add onions, carrots and mushrooms, cooking gently until nearly tender. Mix with rice. Beat eggs, milk and seasonings together. Pour over the rice mixture, place in two medium large casseroles. Dot with butter. Bake for one hour at 325°F.

This can be prepared a day before, with the milk-egg-seasonings added just before baking.

TURKEY CASSEROLE 20

Serves 24

1 — 12 pound Turkey, cooked
or
6-8 pounds chicken breasts, cooked
4 cups chopped celery
2 1/2 cups chopped onion
3 green peppers, sliced
5 cans whole mushrooms — reserve liquid
2 cans water chestnuts, sliced
1/2 pound butter
1 can consomme
2 small cans pimento

Cut turkey or chicken in medium sized pieces and place in 1 very large baking pan or 2 large casseroles. Melt butter in 2 frying pans and cook celery and onion until soft but not brown. Add green pepper and drained mushrooms. Add consomme and water chestnuts and simmer a few minutes. Place with drained pimento into baking pan containing turkey.

Sauce: In large saucepan heat
8 cups of liquid made up of:
any stock from cooking turkey or chicken
liquid from canned mushrooms
cans of consomme (5 or 6)

Add:
2 large cans mushroom soup
1 teaspoon Tabasco sauce
2 envelopes Bovril beef
    bouillon powder
salt and white pepper to taste

Mix together:
1/2 pound butter
1 1/4 cups flour

To this paste add some of hot liquid. Mix until smooth, then add to saucepan, stirring to blend. Cook until sauce thickens. Pour over casserole ingredients, blending well.

Prepare ahead to this point. Refrigerate until an hour before cooking time.

Bake 350ºF for 1 hour or until hot and bubbly.

Serve with Barley Pilaf or rice. May also be used in patty shells in which case cut all ingredients in smaller pieces.

For a more casual occasion, top with freshly baked biscuits.

21   WILD FOWL PIE

Serves 24

Enough pastry for 3 or 4 single crusts
10 frozen, assorted, wild birds
3 bay leaves
12 peppercorns
water

2 cups flour
2 teaspoons thyme
2 teaspoons marjoram
2 teaspoons rosemary
1 Tablespoon salt
1 cup butter, more or less
10 medium sized onions, quartered
8 cups frozen baby carrots
4 cups frozen green beans (not frenched)
3 — 10 ounce cans cream of mushroom soup
3 — 10 ounce cans cream of celery soup
6 — 10 ounce cans (i.e. equal quantity)
   poultry poaching liquid
2 cups white wine
1 cup chopped parsley

Rinse, cut but do not bother to defrost the fowl — skinned ducks, pheasant, dickie birds or a small goose if you have it. Bake in a large covered roaster with the bay leaves and peppercorns in about 2 inches of water for 2 or 3 hours at 350°F. Remove birds as they become tender. Check after 1 hour. Skim, strain and save the liquid. Debone and skin the cooked birds, cutting breasts into 2 or 3 slices but leaving thighs or drumsticks whole, if they are shapely. It is always a treat to come across a good looking leg!

Dredge the meat generously in a paper bag containing the flour, spices and salt. Brown the meat in a large skillet using the butter as needed. Do the last succulent scraps in the last of the butter. Put all of the meat back into the roaster, because it will be large enough for combining the ingredients. Parboil the vegetables to barely tender. Drain and place with the browned meat. Combine canned soups with equal parts of strained poultry juices (make up with extra chicken stock if necessary). Add the wine and parsley, then fold into the meat and vegetables. Ladle the mixture into 2 or 3 large casseroles (or 2 foil pans if you plan to hold in the freezer, in which case defrost before baking). Cover each casserole with a pastry crust, slashing crust 3 or 4 times. Bake at 450°F for 15 minutes, then 325°F for 1 hour, or until crust is crisp and golden.

AVOCADO CREPES WITH CRAB FILLING

Serves 24

Crepes:
1 cup mashed avocado
8 eggs
3/4 cup flour
1/2 teaspoon salt
3/4 cup milk
3/4 cup water

Blend the ingredients, and let stand an hour before cooking. Use butter if you are making crepes in a skillet. This makes 24.

Filling:
1/4 cup butter
6 Tablespoons flour
2 1/2 cups milk
1/2 cup cream
1/4 pound Swiss cheese
1 teaspoon Worcestershire sauce
salt
pepper
2 pounds crabmeat, cooked

Prepare the cream sauce, with butter, flour, milk and cream. Add cubed cheese and stir until thick and smooth. Fold in the 'Wooster', salt, pepper, and flaked crab meat.

Assemble crepes with filling, and arrange in single layer or two buttered baking dishes. Sprinkle with grated Swiss cheese, and dot with butter. At this point you may foilwrap and freeze. When ready to serve you may bake, still wrapped in foil, at 400°F for 15 minutes, remove foil and bake 15 minutes longer.

If unfrozen, bake at 400°F for 15 minutes.

The crepes are very fragile but a beautiful color and flavor and well worth the time.

23 BATTER FOR CREPES

Makes 24

1 1/2 cups milk
6 eggs
3 cups sifted flour
1 teaspoon salt
1/4 cup butter, melted

Blend ingredients until smooth. Allow batter to rest an hour before cooking. Cook crepes on crepe maker, or heavy skillet. It is not necessary to brown both sides.

Crepes may be frozen, stacked with waxed paper between, or frozen with fillings and ready to re-heat and serve.

24 BEAUTIFUL BRUNCH

This is a 24-layer entree — Spectacular to serve and just as good to eat. It looks like a many layered cake.

Serves 24

I *Two recipes of Basic Batter for Crepes:*
Using a 10" coated frying pan with curved sides, make twenty-four 10" crepes.

Stack between pieces of waxed paper until needed.

Note: It is easy to flip the crepes with your hands.

II *Basic Sauce:*
3/4 cup butter
1 cup flour
8 1/4 cups hot milk
1 1/2 teaspoons salt
1 cup whipping cream
3 cups grated Gruyere cheese

Melt butter, stir in flour and simmer a few seconds. Quickly blend in the milk and salt. Cook until sauce thickens and raw flour taste has disappeared. Blend in remaining ingredients. Set aside.

III *Florentine Filling:*
6 large green onions, tops as well
1/3 cup butter
1 teaspoon salt
6 cups chopped cooked spinach,
    well drained
1/4 cup minced parsley

(continued)

Gently saute chopped onions in butter. Add salt, spinach and parsley. Cook until all pan juices have evaporated. Blend in 3 cups of basic sauce. Set aside.

IV *Mushroom Filling:*
4 Tablespoons butter
8 cups sliced mushrooms
3 green onions, chopped
2 Tablespoons lemon juice
3 — 8 ounce packages cream cheese
3 eggs
1 1/2 cups basic sauce

Saute mushrooms and green onion in lemon juice and butter until liquid has evaporated. Blend together cream cheese and eggs. Stir mushroom mixture into cream cheese mixture. Add basic sauce. Set aside.

Now — the fun!
Butter bottom of shallow casserole large enough to hold crepes and with space left around edges for extra sauce.

Put a crepe in bottom of casserole.

Spread with mushroom mixture smoothing well to outer edges. Keep it fairly flat in the middle.

Top with next crepe.

Spread with spinach mixture.

Cover with crepes — adding fillings alternately until all crepes and fillings have been used. End with a crepe. Press down firmly.

Can be prepared ahead of time to this point. Refrigerate.

At serving time — bring to room temperature. Pour remaining sauce over all and around sides.

Topping:
6 slices cooked bacon, crumbled
generous sprinkling of Gruyere and Parmesan cheeses

Bake 350°F — 45 minutes or until well heated and sauce is bubbling. Top should be slightly golden.

To serve — cut in wedges with a sharp knife, spooning extra sauce over all.

CREPES WITH SHRIMP FILLING

Serves 24

Cream Sauce:
3/4 cup butter
1 cup flour
7 cups milk
1 cup cream
2 teaspoons salt
pepper
1 teaspoon lemon juice

Shrimp for Filling:
3 pounds shrimp
2 Tablespoons chopped shallots
1/4 cup butter
2 Tablespoons fresh dill

Topping:
1/4 cup bread crumbs
1/4 cup Swiss cheese, grated
3 Tablespoons butter, melted

Make cream sauce. (Melt butter, add flour. Cook and stir. Gradually add milk and cream, and stir until thick. Add remaining seasonings).

To 1/3 of cream sauce, add the shrimp, which has been lightly cooked in butter, with the shallots. Add the dill. Assemble the crepes with the creamed shrimp mixture, placing them in a large, low baking dish which has been lightly coated with cream.

Pour remaining cream sauce evenly over crepes, sprinkle with mixed crumbs, cheese and butter.

All of this can be done in advance. If you freeze at this stage, defrost before proceeding.

Bake in upper third of oven for 15 minutes at 375ºF. Brown under broiler, 3 inches below, for 2 minutes.

BREASTS OF CHICKEN TARRAGON   26

Serves 24

12 large boned chicken breasts, cut in half
24 strips of bacon
Tarragon
2 — 10 ounce cans of cream of mushroom soup
1 1/2 cups sour cream
4 ounces dry sherry

Pound chicken with the back of a chopping knife to flatten.

Sprinkle with tarragon.

Roll neatly and wrap in bacon strips.

Place in baking dish. Mix last three ingredients and pour over chicken.

Bake in a slow oven at 300ºF for 2-2 1/2 hours.

CURRIED FRUIT BAKE   27

Serves 24

2 — 15 ounce cans peach slices
1 — 20 ounce can pineapple tidbits (5 cups)
4 — 10 ounce cans apricot halves
1 cup maraschino cherries
2/3 cup butter
1 1/2 cups brown sugar
8 teaspoons curry powder
2 cups juice from the fruits
2 Tablespoons cornstarch

Drain all the fruits well, reserving 2 cups of the juice. Put in a shallow greased baking dish.

Melt the butter in a medium saucepan. Stir in the sugar and curry powder. Add the reserved juice and bring to a boil, stirring well until all ingredients are well combined. Thicken with cornstarch dissolved in juice or water. Pour sauce over the fruit and bake uncovered for 1 hour at 325ºF.

This can be made ahead of time and refrigerated. To reheat, place in a 350ºF oven for 30 minutes.

Best with ham — good with turkey.

28 SPICED BEEF "A TRADITIONAL OLD ENGLISH RECIPE"

15 pounds round roast, boned
1-1 1/2 pounds Demerara sugar
1 cup non-iodized salt
1 ounce saltpeter
2 ounces white pepper
1 ounce allspice
1/2 ounce ground cloves

Have the butcher cut a high chunky roast (rather than flat and broad), and fill the boned hole with suet.

Stand the meat in a stoneware crock in a very *cool place*. Cover. Rub with the sugar the first two nights.

Add the spices, and rub the beef well everyday for three weeks.

Remove from the crock and wrap the meat in foil. Roast at 300ºF to "rare" on the meat thermometer. Approximately 18 minutes per pound.

Cool in the wrapping, then unwrap and re-crock, with the spice and juices.

Cover with 6 beers until ready to serve.

Store in a cold place.

29 ENGLISH MUSTARD SAUCE

1/2 cup dry mustard
1/2 cup white vinegar
1/2 cup sugar
1/4 teaspoon salt
2 eggs, beaten
1 cup mayonnaise

Shake mustard and vinegar together in a small jar, and let stand for one hour.

Combine mustard mixture with sugar, salt and egg in a small saucepan. Cook over medium heat for 5 minutes, stirring constantly until thickened and almost boiling. Cool. Stir in mayonnaise until smooth.

Store in refrigerator, covered tightly.

PAELLA ESPAÑOLA

Serves 24

6 cups long grain rice, cooked
4 chickens cut in serving pieces
    oven-browned*
2 pounds ham or cooked pork, cubed
1 pound whole shrimp
1 pound crab meat or lobster (optional)
1/2 cup olive oil
3 large onions, chopped
4 garlic cloves, crushed
3 red or green peppers, cut in strips
2 cans (28 ounce) whole tomatoes
3 cups green peas, cooked
1 Tablespoon salt
2 teaspoons powdered saffron
2 lemons, cut in wedges
1 pound (or 1 can) clams or mussels in
    shell cooked (optional)

In a large frying pan, saute the onion and garlic in oil until tender and golden. Add cooked rice, meat, shellfish (not the chicken or mussels) peas, tomatoes, salt and saffron, stirring gently until hot. Transfer to 2 large paella pans (or large baking pans). Distribute the chicken into the rice-vegetable mixture and bake at 350ºF for 30-45 minutes. Garnish with mussels, lemon wedges and pepper strips. Bake 10 more minutes.

. . . a typical Spanish dish, especially enhanced by a Spanish Rosé wine.

Oven browning — place chicken pieces on broiler rack, brush lightly with melted butter and broil until skin is golden brown, turn and do other side. Does not have to be cooked through.

31   LASAGNE

Serves 24

2 pounds lasagne noodles
2 Tablespoons salt
water

3 pounds ground beef
olive oil
2 large onions, chopped
2 cups chopped celery
2 green peppers, chopped
2 cans mushroom bits (drain and
    reserve juice)
2 — 16 ounce cans tomatoes
    (Italian preferred)
2 small cans tomato paste

salt and pepper to taste
1 Tablespoon sweet basil
2 Tablespoons oregano
2 Tablespoons Worcestershire sauce
3 cloves fresh garlic, crushed

2 — 16 ounce cartons cottage cheese
2 — 16 ounce bricks mozzarella cheese
    (cut into chunks)
Parmesan cheese

Brown beef in a little olive oil, add salt, pepper and garlic. Add onion, celery and green pepper. Cook until soft. Add mushrooms, tomatoes, tomato paste, sweet basil and oregano. Simmer for one hour.

Cook lasagne noodles, as package directs, in a large pot, or use a large frying pan so they can cook flat. When tender, drain and spread out on brown paper.

Using 2 large rectangular baking dishes. Assemble the lasagne — a layer of noodles, layer of sauce, cottage cheese, chunks of mozzarella. Repeat layers ending with sauce and sprinkle Parmesan and mozzarella cheese on top. (There should be 3 layers).

Bake in oven at 350°F for one hour.

TORTILLA DELIGHT 32

Serves 24

4 packages (1 dozen each) corn Tortillas
1 1/3 cups salad oil
5 Tablespoons instant minced onion
1 cup water
4 — 16 ounce cans tomato sauce
1 — 6 ounce can tomato paste
4 cups sour cream
12 canned green chilies (chopped)
2 teaspoons garlic salt
4 cups chopped ripe olives
2 pounds grated Monteray Jack cheese
1/2 cup butter

Tear tortillas into bite sized pieces (defrost if frozen). Heat oil in frying pan and fry tortillas until crisp, but not brown; remove from oil and drain. Soak onion in water for 5 minutes; add tomato sauce, tomato paste, sour cream, chilies and garlic salt; stir until well blended. Put half tortillas in buttered 8-10 quart casserole (or use two smaller ones); cover with half tomato mixture, then half the olives and half the cheese. Repeat layers ending with cheese. Dot remaining butter on top. Bake 350°F for 30 minutes.

BAKED WHOLE SALMON OR ARCTIC CHAR 33

Serves 12-16

6-8 pound fish
seasoning salt
onions, sliced
celery, sliced
carrots, sliced
1 cup dry white wine

Place cleaned fish on large piece of oiled heavy duty foil, or baking pan. Sprinkle liberally with seasoning salt. Fill cavity with sliced onions, celery and carrots. Pour dry white wine over. Seal foil completely. Bake 425°F for 10 minutes per one inch thickness of fish, measuring at the thickest spot.

Test fish — it should be opaque and easy to flake, but not dry. Do not turn fish.

Serve hot or cold.

MOUSSAKA

The authentic Greek version. Prepare a day or two ahead and refrigerate. Freezes well too. (If frozen, let thaw completely before reheating).

Serves
20-24

3 pounds lean ground beef
1 large onion, minced
1 teaspoon seasoned salt
2 teaspoons salt
2 teaspoons pepper
1 teaspoon cinnamon
1 teaspoon tomato paste
1/2 can (14 ounces) tomatoes, blended

Saute beef with onion and seasonings. Add tomato paste and canned tomatoes and cook gently until almost all liquid has evaporated. Set aside.

3 eggplants cut in thick rounds, unpeeled
2 zucchini cut in 1" rounds, unpeeled
4 potatoes sliced thin

Fry vegetables in deep hot oil until well browned, a few pieces at a time. Drain on paper towels or brush vegetable slices with oil and brown under broiler — turning to brown both sides.

Thick White Sauce:
3/4 pound margarine or butter
1 cup flour
1 1/2 litres whole milk
2 egg yolks
1 teaspoon salt
2 cups grated Parmesan cheese

Melt margarine or butter in deep saucepan. Whisk in flour and salt.

Add milk gradually, whisking constantly. Cook until medium thick. Beat in egg yolks.

In two large casseroles or rectangular lasagne pans at least 3" or 4" deep, arrange a layer of potatoes, then meat sauce, eggplant and zucchini and another layer of meat sauce.

Pour white sauce over all. Sprinkle Parmesan cheese evenly over both casseroles. Bake 350ºF, approximately 45 minutes. Let stand 15 minutes before cutting.

Serves 30

9 pounds sirloin or chuck steak, cubed
4 green peppers diced
4 cans mushrooms with liquid
2 2/3 cups red wine
1 1/2 cans (8 ounces each) tomato paste
3 envelopes dry onion soup mix
2 1/2 Tablespoons Worcestershire sauce
1 1/2 teaspoons oregano
2 bay leaves
1/2 teaspoon turmeric
1/2 teaspoon garlic powder
a few grindings of pepper
1/3 cup flour
2 cups water
2 1/2 cups sour cream

Brown the meat in a little oil, a few pieces at a time.

Then saute the green pepper and mushrooms. Place in a large Dutch oven.

Combine the remaining ingredients except for the flour and water and pour over the meat, peppers and mushrooms.

If necessary, add more water to not quite cover meat.

Cover tightly and simmer until the meat is fork tender.

This will vary with the cut of meat used.

Combine the flour and water. Add some of the meat juices to the flour and water paste, then blend into hot meat mixture, stirring quickly.

May be held at this point. Just before serving, stir in the sour cream.

Reheat over low heat. Do not allow to boil as sour cream will separate.

Serve over buttered noodles or rice.

This recipe can be made ahead and frozen, following the main cooking period and prior to adding the sour cream.

36   SEAFOOD CASSEROLE

*Serves
25-30*

6·cups cooked wild rice
1 cup uncooked white rice
3 small onions, chopped
4 1/2 cups celery, chopped
6 cans shrimp (drained)
6 cans lobster (drained)
3 cans crab (drained)
3 cans large button mushrooms (drained)
3 small cans pimento, sliced
6 cans mushroom soup (or 3 large)

Mix all together in large casserole and bake at 325ºF until heated through, about 1 hour.

Note: 6 cans lobster can be replaced by 3 cans lobster and 3 cans chicken haddie.

37   CHICKEN CERRITO

Serves 24

24 pieces frying chickens (combination
    of thighs, breasts, and legs)
2 lemons, cut into halves
4 cloves garlic, minced
3 teaspoons tarragon
2 teaspoons thyme
1 teaspoon salt
1 teaspoon pepper
3 tins cream of chicken soup
1 cup cream
1 cup dry white Vermouth
2 cups grated Parmesan cheese
1 — 14 ounce tin sliced, pitted black olives

Rub each piece of chicken with the cut lemon. Lay out on large roasting pan, and sprinkle with herb mixture of garlic, tarragon, thyme, salt and pepper. Cover and refrigerate until baking time. Bake uncovered at 350ºF for 45 minutes.

Blend the soup, cream, Vermouth, and half of the Parmesan. Pour the sauce over the chicken. Bake and baste for 30 minutes. Sprinkle with remaining cheese and olives, and bake 30 minutes more.

Serve with parslied egg noodles or one of the fine Italian pastas.

WILD DUCK WITH WHITE GRAPES

Serves
20-24

10 large wild ducks
10 Tablespoons butter
10 stalks celery
salt
freshly ground black pepper
2 teaspoons dried rosemary
2 teaspoons dried basil
2 teaspoons dried marjoram
2 teaspoons dried thyme
chicken or beef stock
Thompson seedless grapes

Rub duck breasts with butter, salt and pepper. Chill or hold refrigerated overnight or for several hours.

Put celery and a few grapes in the cavity of each duck.

Sprinkle evenly with herb mixture. Place in a roasting pan and roast in a 450°F oven for 15 minutes. Pour stock into pan, turn oven to 300°F. Cook approximately 2 hours longer basting ducks with sauce during the last half hour.

Sauce:
In a saucepan over medium heat, melt:
1 cup red currant jelly
juice of one lemon
very finely grated rind of one lemon
    and one orange
1 Tablespoon prepared mustard
1 clove garlic minced
1/2 teaspoon salt
1 cup dry sherry

Baste ducks with this mixture two or three times in the last 1/2 hour. Dissolve 2 teaspoons cornstarch in 2 Tablespoons cold water. Stir into remaining sauce. Simmer two minutes. Add 4 Tablespoons Grand Marnier. Remove ducks to heated serving platter, cut them into serving pieces. Discard celery. Put cooked grapes into sauce, pour sauce over ducks. Garnish platter with large clusters of fresh grapes. Serve.

39 BAKED PORK MEDALLIONS

Serves 24

9 pounds pork tenderloin
3 — 10 ounce cans cream of chicken soup
3 — 10 ounce cans cream of mushroom soup
1 — 10 ounce can cream of celery soup
1 — 10 ounce can consomme
4 — 10 ounce cans mushrooms, drained
1 tin chopped pimento, drained
2 packages onion soup mix
1 Tablespoon Worcestershire sauce

Cut pork tenderloin in medallions, 1/2 inch thick, allowing 4 per person. In a large casserole or baking dish mix all remaining ingredients. Add medallions and cover with the sauce. Bake 250°F for 5 hours.

40 BARLEY PILAF

Serves 26

1 large onion, chopped
1 green pepper, chopped (optional)
6 Tablespoons butter or beef fat
1 package pearl barley (900 grams,
    or 4 1/2 cups)
3 cans mushroom pieces, including juice
3 — 10 ounce cans consomme or beef juices
1 Tablespoon salt

Brown the onion and green pepper in three Tablespoons butter or fat. Set aside in large casserole. Brown the barley in the remaining fat and add to the large casserole. Add salt, consomme and mix.

Bake, covered, about 2 hours at 350°F. If re-heating, more meat juices, vegetable liquid or water may be added.

An added touch — at serving time sprinkle with toasted pine-nuts.

VEAL MARENGO

Serves 12
can be
doubled

4 pounds shoulder or leg of veal
   (or tender beef)
1 Tablespoon olive or salad oil
1 small clove garlic
1 pound mushrooms, sliced
24 tiny white onions, or 4 medium onions, sliced
1 cup sliced small carrots
3 Tablespoons flour
1 1/2 teaspoons salt
1/2 teaspoon pepper
2 cups tomato sauce
1 cup dry white wine
2 cups chicken broth
1 herb bouquet (2 stalks celery with leaves,
   sprigs of parsley, 1/2 teaspoon
   rosemary, 1 bay leaf — tied in a
   cheesecloth bag.)

Trim fat from meat, cut in 1 1/2 inch cubes. Heat oil in large skillet with garlic, which is later removed. Add veal in small amounts and brown. Place in casserole. Cook mushrooms, onions and carrots gently in skillet, adding a little oil if required. Spoon vegetables over veal. Stir flour, salt and pepper into pan juices, then tomato sauce, broth and wine. Cook until thick, stirring constantly. Place herb bouquet in casserole with meat. Pour the sauce over the mixture. Cover and bake in pre-heated 350ºF oven for 1 1/2 hours, or until veal is tender.

Freezes well. Thaw before reheating, as veal will shrink.

SAUCY BAKED BEANS

Serves 24

6 — 16 ounce cans of pork and beans
   in tomato sauce
2 medium onions, chopped (1 cup)
2 green peppers, diced
1/2 cup packed brown sugar
1/2 cup catsup
4 Tablespoons Worcestershire sauce
6 slices of bacon

In a four quart casserole combine all ingredients, except bacon. Place bacon on the top. Bake uncovered for 1 1/2 hours at 350ºF.

43   STRAWBERRIES ROMANOFF

Serves 24

6 pints washed strawberries
   (leave stems on)
10 egg yolks
2 cups berry sugar
2 cups good sherry or any favorite
   liqueur
2 cups whipping cream, whipped

In a double boiler beat egg yolks, until creamy and lemon colored. Gradually add sugar, beating constantly. Fold in the sherry; stir over hot water until mixture thickens. Pour into a china or glass bowl to cool. Before serving fold in the whipped cream.

To serve, place the bowls of berries and the Romanoff on the serving table. Guests may use the sauce as a dip, in hand; from their plates, or spoon the sauce over the berries on their plates.

44   SWEDISH ALMOND CREAM RING

Serves 24

3/4 pound ground almonds
1 1/2 cups sugar
3 cups light cream
2 1/4 Tablespoons unflavored gelatine
3/8 cup water
3 cups whipping cream, whipped
pinch of salt
1 teaspoon almond flavoring
sweetened fresh or frozen fruit, or
   strawberries, well drained, or
   canned fruit, drained and chilled

Combine almonds, sugar and light cream in saucepan. Bring to boiling point and simmer 5 minutes. Soften gelatine in water for five minutes, and stir into cream mixture until dissolved. Cool until mixture mounds. Add salt, and flavoring to whipped cream, then fold into cooled almond mixture. Spoon into 12 cup ring mould. Allow to set.

Invert on platter to serve, filling with drained fruit.

CHOCOLATE MOUSSE CREPES   45

Serves 24

12 ounces semi-sweet chocolate
6 Tablespoons sugar
6 Tablespoons water
6 egg yolks
3 cups cream, whipped
48 small (5") or 24 large dessert crepes

Melt the chocolate, and blend in the sugar and water in double boiler. Add beaten egg yolks gradually, stirring until smooth and thickened. Cool to room temperature. Then blend chocolate mixture into the whipped cream.

Put a spoonful or two of chocolate filling on each crepe; roll and place seam down on serving tray. The crepes freeze well at this point, but should be defrosted before serving.

Serve with hot chocolate sauce, if desired.

Hot Chocolate Sauce:

12 ounces semi-sweet chocolate*
2 Tablespoons cream
4 Tablespoons cognac, rum or coffee liqueur

Melt chocolate over hot water, in double-boiler, thin with cream, stir in liqueur. Drizzle over crepes at serving time.

*You're overstocked with Easter eggs and all that chocolate the kids sell for school projects — melt those baseballs, hockey pucks and almond bars in with the semi-sweet — that's this recipe's secret ingredient!

46 DAIQUIRI SOUFFLÉ

Serves 24

10 eggs, separated
2 1/2 cups sugar
2 grated rinds of lemons (large)
2 grated rinds of limes (large)
2/3 cup *fresh* lemon juice
2/3 cup *fresh* lime juice
1/2 teaspoon salt
2 1/2 Tablespoons gelatine
2/3 cup white rum
3 cups whipping cream
food coloring
chocolate curls
toasted almonds, chopped

Beat egg yolks until light and fluffy. Gradually add 1 1/4 cups sugar, beating constantly. Add grated peels, juices and salt. Beat well. In a heavy saucepan over very low heat, cook and stir constantly until mixture thickens slightly.

Sprinkle gelatine over rum, let stand 5 minutes, then stir into hot custard until dissolved. Cool. Color pale green if desired using about 3 drops green and 2 drops yellow food coloring.

Beat egg whites until foamy. Gradually beat in remaining 1 1/4 cups sugar. Beat until stiff.

Beat *2 cups* of cream until stiff. Fold egg whites into custard, then fold in whipped cream.

Pour into 2 souffle dishes and chill or freeze. To serve, top with chocolate curls and slivered almonds. Decorate with remaining 1 cup of cream, whipped.

47 ICE CREAM CAKE

Serves 24

4 or more pints ice cream, any
    flavor or flavors
1 package vanilla wafers
2 cups chocolate syrup
1 cup maraschino cherries
4 crushed toffee bars
1 cup whipping cream

Line bottom and sides of buttered spring-form pan with vanilla wafers. Size of pan is optional. A very large spring-form pan will slice to 24 servings.

(continued)

Cover vanilla wafers with scoops of ice cream. Drizzle with 1/2 chocolate syrup, 1/2 of the cherries, and 1/2 of the crushed toffee.

Repeat with the remaining ice cream, chocolate, cherries and toffee. Top with vanilla wafers and freeze the cake.

Remove cake 15-30 minutes before serving and ice with whipped cream if desired. Garnish with shaved chocolate and cherries.

SUMMER FRUIT IN WINE   48

Serves 24

2 honeydew melons
10 pounds watermelon
1 quart strawberries
1 quart blueberries (fresh)
1 pound seedless green grapes
5 oranges
2 grapefruit
2 peaches
2 apples
1 bottle Sweet White Wine
    (such as Lindeman's Pearl
    or Kaiser Pearl)
2 bananas

Cut the honeydew melon and watermelon in cubes or balls. Rinse strawberries. Drain well and hull, but do not cut. (They will lose their color). Rinse and pick over blueberries. Rinse and stem grapes. Peel and section oranges and grapefruit. Peel and slice peaches. Slice apples evenly, leaving peel on.

Combine in large bowl. There will be at least 24 cups of fruit. Pour wine over, using enough to coat the fruit, especially the apples and peaches, or they will darken. Refrigerate several hours, covered tightly.

Immediately before serving, slice the bananas and fold in gently.

49   KENTUCKY DERBY PIE

Serves 8-10

1 — 9 inch unbaked pie shell
1/4 cup butter
1 cup white sugar
3 eggs, beaten
3/4 cup white corn syrup
1 teaspoon salt
1 teaspoon vanilla
1/2 cup chocolate chips
1/2 cup chopped pecans
2 Tablespoons Kentucky bourbon
   (Rye can be used but bourbon is best)

Cream butter, and add sugar gradually. Add beaten eggs, corn syrup, salt and vanilla. Mix well. Add chocolate chips, nuts and bourbon. Stir until well mixed and pour into pie crust.

Bake in pre-heated oven 375°F for 60 minutes or until centre is set. Rewarm to serve. Serve with sweetened whipped cream, flavored with vanilla.

Can be frozen after baking.

50   CANDIED ALMONDS

2 cups whole almonds blanched
1 cup sugar
4 Tablespoons butter
1 teaspoon vanilla
1 1/2 teaspoons salt

Heat almonds, sugar and butter in a heavy skillet over medium heat, stirring constantly until almonds are toasted and sugar is a golden color. This may take up to 15 minutes. Remove from heat and add vanilla. Immediately spread nuts on aluminum foil, separating the nuts from each other, then quickly sprinkle with salt.

Cool.

Break into 1-2 nut clusters. Store in airtight jar.

This is *so special*.

Heirlooms

Top picture:	(in a clockwise
	direction)
	Oysters in a Breadbox
	My Grandmother's Chutney
	Calico Mustard Pickle Relish
	Mustard Pickle
	Old Irish Marmalade
Bottom picture:	1933 Gingersnaps
	Brown Sugar Pound Cake

BEEF VEGETABLE SOUP   51

1 very meaty soup bone, or left over roast
    beef bones with meat
1 large onion, cut in half
2 bay leaves
3 celery stalks with leaves — left whole
1 clove garlic

Put above ingredients in a large pot, with about 3 1/2 quarts of water. Cover, bring to a boil, then let simmer 3 1/2 hours. Remove bone, bay leaves, garlic. Cool and skim off froth and fat. Chop celery, leaves and onions and return to stock. Remove meat from bones, add to stock.

Add the following:

1 — 16 ounce can tomatoes
3 carrots, sliced
1 onion, quartered
1 handful macaroni, or 1 1/2 cups uncooked
    egg noodles
2 cups sliced celery
1 Tablespoon soya sauce
1 teaspoon thyme
salt and pepper to taste

Left over vegetables, such as cabbage, turnip, beans may be added also.

Simmer another hour, then correct seasonings. This soup is better if made ahead, and not served immediately.

HAM AND PEA SOUP   52

6 to 8 quarts water
Ham bone (from cooked ham) with some meat
    still on it
1 pound dried split peas
1 medium onion, diced
3 stalks celery, diced, including leaves
3 carrots, diced

Simmer water and ham bone together, covered, 3-4 hours till meat falls off the bone. Remove bone. Dice ham and return to soup kettle with rest of ingredients.

Simmer slowly till desired consistency is obtained. Should be quite thick. Adjust seasonings. Depending on saltiness of ham, use seasoning salt, pepper, basil, parsley, etc.

Serves 8 very hungry people.

53 SPRING BORSCH

Serves
8-10

10 young beets, stalks and leaves
6 cups (or to cover) water or chicken stock
2 teaspoons salt
1 onion, diced
2 Tablespoons parsley
2 Tablespoons lemon juice
1/2 cup broad beans
2 garlic cloves, diced
2 Tablespoons chopped dill
1/2 cup peas
1/2 cup beans
1/2 cup potatoes, diced
1 Tablespoon sugar
1 cup sour cream or sweet cream

Scrub the beets but do not peel. Rinse leaves and stalks. Set leaves aside, dice beets and stalks. Add water, salt and lemon juice. Bring to a boil, add shredded leaves and rest of vegetables. Do not overcook. When vegetables are just tender, add cream and serve.

54 OYSTERS IN A BREAD BOX (A LUNCHEON OR SUPPER DISH)

1 loaf French bread
1/2 cup melted butter
2 dozen oysters
1/2 cup cream
dash of Tabasco, cayenne pepper, salt
   and pepper.

Cut off top of French loaf and hollow out center. Brush inside of loaf with melted butter.

Fry oysters, a few at at time, in butter until edges curl.

Reserve liquor from frying and add 1/2 cup cream and spices.

Return oysters to pan and cook until done.

Fill the loaf with this mixture, put on top crust and brush the loaf with a little cream and cayenne pepper.

Place on cookie sheet. Bake for 20 minutes 375°F.

Slice and serve hot.

TURNIP SOUFFLÉ

Serves 8
4 cups mashed, cooked turnips
2 cups soft bread crumbs
1/2 cup melted butter
2 Tablespoons brown sugar
2 teaspoons salt
4 eggs, slightly beaten

Mix and place in greased casserole. Dot with butter. Bake at 350°F for one hour.

Also good made with squash. May be made ahead of time.

SCOTTISH DRESSING FOR TURKEY

— has been used by at least five generations.
For every 2 cups of dressing needed, mix together:
1 cup dry bread crumbs
1 cup oatmeal, not rolled oats
1 Tablespoon savory
1 teaspoon sage
1/2 teaspoon salt
1/2 cup chopped onions
1/2 cup butter

Saute onions in butter. Add to rest of ingredients. Pack into both cavities of turkey.

Note: if using pre-basted turkeys, scoop butter out of cavity and use it for the stuffing.

57   HAM LOAF

Serves 12

2 pounds of ground ham
1 1/2 pounds of ground pork
1 cup of dry bread crumbs
1 cup milk
2 slightly beaten eggs

Glaze:
3/4 cup brown sugar
1/2 teaspoon powdered cloves
1/2 teaspoon dry mustard

Combine first five ingredients, mix well.

Mix sugar, cloves and mustard.

Grease lightly a 10 x 5 x 3 inch loaf pan.

Spread brown sugar mix in bottom of loaf pan. Then pack meat mixture on top.

Bake in 350ºF oven 1 1/2 hours.

To serve, invert on platter and loaf will be self-glazed.

Serve with mustard sauce.

58   MUSTARD SAUCE

2 egg yolks, beaten
1 Tablespoon sugar
3 Tablespoons prepared mustard
2 Tablespoons vinegar
1 Tablespoon water
3/4 teaspoon salt
1 Tablespoon butter
1 Tablespoon horseradish
1/2 cup whipping cream, whipped

To egg yolks, add sugar, mustard, vinegar, water and salt. Mix well.

Cook over simmering water, stirring constantly, until thick — about 5 minutes.

Blend in horseradish and butter.

Cool.

Fold in whipped cream.

Serves
8-10

3 pounds tender stewing beef, cut in
    1 inch cubes
2 Tablespoons fat
2 or 3 large onions, sliced
2 garlic cloves, minced
1 cup chopped celery, with some leaves
1/2 cup parsley, chopped
2 1/2 cups canned tomatoes
1 bay leaf, crumbled
1/2 teaspoon thyme
1/2 teaspoon marjoram
4 teaspoons salt
1/4 teaspoon dry mustard
freshly ground black pepper
2 1/2 cups water
3 or 4 medium carrots
1/3-1/2 small turnip
4 or 5 medium potatoes, quartered
1/4 cup flour
3/4 cup water

Brown meat well in fat in large Dutch oven or heavy pan. Add sliced onions, garlic, celery, parsley, tomatoes, bay leaf, thyme, marjoram, salt, pepper and 2 1/2 cups water. Bring to a boil, reduce heat, cover and simmer 2 hours or bake in 325°F oven.

Cut carrots in approximately one inch pieces, turnips a little smaller and add, along with potatoes and cook for 40-50 minutes longer. Blend flour with 3/4 cup cold water (use 2 or 3 tablespoons more flour if you like gravy to be quite thick). Add a little hot stew to water and flour mixture then stir into stew. Cook for 10 minutes.

This can be made in the morning and reheated . . . it tastes even better the second day. Freezes well without potatoes.

60 OLD FASHIONED BARBECUED SPARE RIBS

Serves 6

5 pounds lean spare ribs
2 Tablespoons fat from ribs
1 large onion, chopped
2 Tablespoons vinegar
4 Tablespoons lemon juice
2 Tablespoons brown sugar
1/8 teaspoon cayenne pepper
1 teaspoon prepared horseradish
1 cup tomato ketchup
3 Tablespoons Worcestershire sauce
1 cup water
2 teaspoons dry mustard
1/2 cup chopped celery
1 clove garlic, chopped

Brown ribs in hot oven or under broiler. Measure 2 Tablespoons of fat from ribs into skillet and saute onions. Add vinegar, lemon juice, brown sugar, cayenne, horseradish, ketchup, Worcestershire sauce, water, mustard, celery and garlic. Cook until sauce is hot and smooth. Place ribs in baking pan. Pour sauce over ribs. Bake in moderate oven at 350°F for 1 1/2 hours, or until tender. Baste occasionally.

61 MA'S BAKING POWDER BISCUITS

Makes 12-15

2 cups flour
1 Tablespoon baking powder
1 Tablespoon sugar
1/4 cup butter
dash salt
3/4 cup milk
1 egg

Mix dry ingredients. Cut in butter until mixture resembles cornmeal. Stir egg into milk. Mix lightly into dry mixture. Turn out onto floured board and knead 12 times. Pat out and cut into circles. Bake on cookie pan 425°F for 12-15 minutes or until golden brown.

Serve hot with Chicken Pot Pie.

CHICKEN POT PIE 62

Serves
8-10

3-4 cups cooked chicken (or turkey),
cut into bite-sized pieces

Sauce to cover. Can use chicken stock, leftover gravy, thin cream sauce. If desperate use cream of chicken soup.

1 cup sliced carrots, cooked
1 cup mushrooms, canned or fresh
1 cup small peas
1 small onion, diced
1/2 cup green pepper chunks

Place above ingredients in greased casserole. Heat at 350ºF until bubbly. Meanwhile make one recipe baking powder biscuits. Arrange some on top of chicken, bake remainder separately. Return casserole to 425ºF oven until biscuits are nicely browned.

Variations:
1. To jazz this up, add white wine to gravy.
2. Use whatever leftover vegetables on hand — broccoli, green beans. Diced pimento adds color.
3. Biscuit dough can be used to make a crust, rather than individual biscuits.
4. Can be made in individual ramekins.

HOLLY WREATH SALAD 63

1 small package lime Jello
1 cup hot water
1 small tub cottage cheese
3 carrots, shredded
3 stalks celery, diced
1 small onion, grated
1/2 cup cream
1/2 cup mayonnaise

Dissolve Jello in hot water. Chill. When partially set, stir in sieved cottage cheese and other ingredients. Pour into well oiled ring mold. When set, unmold onto serving plate. Ring with parsley sprigs and tomato wedges.

64   BOSTON BAKED BEANS

Serves 8

4 or 5 ounces salt pork
3 cups pea beans
3/4 cup brown sugar
2 teaspoons dry mustard
1 1/2 Tablespoons salt
2/3 cup molasses
1 peeled onion

The night before, soak 3 cups beans in cold water to cover. In the morning, drain off water and put in large pot. Cover with cold water. Bring to boil and simmer, cook until tender. Put a small peeled onion in bottom of bean pot. Drain beans (reserving about 1 cup of liquid) and pour around onion in pot. Mix brown sugar, mustard, salt and molasses together and pour around beans, add enough bean liquid to just cover. Cut salt pork into small pieces and push down into beans. Bake at least 5 hours at 300°F. Keep covered. Check beans occasionally, push down with spoon, adding reserved liquid only if necessary. Do not stir, or beans will get mushy.

65   GLAZING A NEW YEAR'S HAM

1 large ham with some fat on it.

Remove hot ham from oven. With a sharp knife, score all over in 1-inch diamonds. Put whole cloves in each diamond. Coat ham generously with white corn syrup and spread with the following:

Mix:
2 cups fine dry bread crumbs
2 cups brown sugar
2 teaspoons dry mustard
white vinegar to moisten

Place ham in 500°F oven for 15 minutes. Baste now and then. Remove from oven and decorate with pineapple chunks and halved, candied cherries. If there is a length of bone standing out, dress it up with a white paper frill.

Serves 8

3 pounds fillet of sole
2 onions, sliced
2 bay leaves
1 1/2 teaspoons salt
2 cups dry white wine or a little less
    dry white Vermouth
3 Tablespoons butter
2 Tablespoons flour
1 teaspoon lemon juice
4 egg yolks
1/2 pound shrimp meat
1/4 pound prawn tails or additional shrimp
1/4 pound mushrooms sauteed in butter
1 ounce grated Parmesan cheese

Put sliced onions, crumbled bay leaves, salt and wine in a pan, then add the fillets of sole.

Put pan in heated oven (375°F) for 10 minutes.

Remove fillets and strain pan juices.

Melt butter and mix with the flour and juices from the fish pan — boil down to a thick sauce. Add lemon juice and egg yolks and simmer gently. Stir shrimp and prawns into sauce and add sauteed mushrooms. Pour over fillets in casserole, sprinkle with grated cheese, return to oven for 15 minutes or until top is light brown.

67 STEAMED BOSTON BROWN BREAD

1 cup corn meal
1 cup rye flour
1 cup graham flour
3/4 Tablespoon baking soda
1 teaspoon salt

2 cups sour milk
3/4 cup molasses
1 cup raisins

Mix dry ingredients together. Make a well in the middle and add molasses and sour milk. Blend well. Stir in raisins. Pour into buttered steamer mold 2/3 full. Cover tightly.* *

Steam 3 1/2 hours. This may be made ahead and reheated by steaming for 1/2 hour.

Variation:
1 cup Brex breakfast cereal or 1 cup whole wheat flour may be used interchangeably with rye and graham flour.

* *If you have a proper steamer, it will have its own cover. If not, use a heavy ironstone bowl, cover tightly with a double layer of foil, tied down around the rim.

Try this with Jean's Beans, Boston Baked Beans.

68 OATMEAL MUFFINS

2/3 cup plus
    2 Tablespoons brown sugar
3 Tablespoons melted butter
1 egg
1 cup flour
1 cup oatmeal
1 1/2 teaspoons soda
1/4 teaspoon salt
1/3 cup coarsely chopped dates
1 cup sour milk

Blend first three ingredients. Mix together all remaining dry ingredients. Add to first mixture, along with sour milk. Fill greased muffin pans 2/3 full. Bake 375° F 25-30 minutes. Makes 1 dozen large, sweet muffins.

TUCK SHOP BUNS
UNIVERSITY OF ALBERTA

2 packages instant yeast
1/2 cup warm water
1 Tablespoon sugar

Dissolve sugar in water. Soften yeast in it.

In a mixing bowl blend:
2 cups boiling water
2 Tablespoons margarine or butter
1 teaspoon salt
2 Tablespoons sugar
2 eggs, beaten
4 1/2 cups flour

Let cool. Add softened yeast.

Beat mixture hard for 5-8 minutes to form smooth dough. Cover and let stand in warm place to rise for about one hour or until dough has doubled in bulk.

To make buns:
1 cup butter or margarine
2 cups sugar
4 teaspoons cinnamon

In flat bowl melt margarine or butter. Set aside to cool. In another flat bowl mix sugar and cinnamon. Turn raised dough on to lightly floured board. Cut dough into pieces the size of an orange. Dip first in melted butter or margarine, then into cinnamon mixture. Stretch dough and tie in simple knot. Place on greased pan. Let rise 45 minutes. Bake 375°F-400°F for 30-40 minutes.

N.B. This is a very sticky dough, but do not add extra flour as it spoils the buns.

The Tuck Shop was demolished years ago to make room for new buildings, but the memories linger on.

BLUEBERRY MUFFINS (DATES BACK TO 1880)

Yields: 15

1/3 cup shortening
1/2 cup brown sugar
1 egg
1 1/2 cups flour
1 teaspoon baking powder
1/2 teaspoon baking soda
1/2 teaspoon cinnamon
1/4 teaspoon nutmeg
1/2 teaspoon salt
1/2 cup sour milk
1 cup fresh blueberries (folded in last)

Beat together the shortening, sugar and egg. Mix in the other ingredients, then add blueberries. Bake in greased muffin tins 400°F for 25-30 minutes.

Lemon Sauce for Blueberry Muffins:
1 lemon (juice and grated rind)
3/4 cup sugar
1 Tablespoon cornstarch
1 cup cold water
1 egg
2 Tablespoons butter
pinch of salt

Mix sugar and cornstarch and salt. Add egg and melted butter; mix well. Add water, and grated rind. Place in double boiler and stir until thickened. Add lemon juice after sauce is cooked and removed from stove.

Pour sauce over hot muffins and serve.

PLUM LOAF
A CHRISTMAS TRADITION OF
NOVA SCOTIAN ORIGIN

This is moist and heavy.

> 2 cups warm water
> 2 Tablespoons dry granular yeast
> 2 teaspoons sugar
> 5 cups milk
> 5 cups water
> 1 1/2 cups sugar
> 1 pound lard
> 2 Tablespoons salt
> 24 cups all-purpose flour plus about 8 more
> 8 pounds sultana raisins

Mix first three ingredients and let stand 10-15 minutes until yeast is dissolved. Scald milk, add warm water and sugar, stir to dissolve. Melt and cool lard and add to milk with salt. Blend in yeast mixture. Gradually beat in 24 cups flour (a canning kettle is a good container). Add the raisins and press them in well. Knead on floured table top, adding as much more flour as is needed to make a *stiff* dough. Knead until smooth and elastic. Place in a greased pot and butter top of dough. Let rise until doubled. Punch down and let rise again until doubled. Punch down and divide into 10 balls. Shape into round loaves and place on greased cookie sheets. Plum loaf is round and crusty and not very high. Let rise again. Bake 375°F 45-60 minutes — until bottom of loaf "rings hollow" when tapped. Brush tops with melted butter while hot.

Great with cold turkey or toasted on Christmas morning.

Everyone knows at least nine friends and relatives to give a loaf to.

Wrap loaves with red ribbons and sprigs of holly.

72 HIGHLAND SCONES

1 cup sugar
3 cups sifted flour
2 teaspoons cream of tartar
1 teaspoon soda
1/2 teaspoon salt
1/2 cup raisins (cover with hot water
    for 5 minutes and drain)
2 Tablespoons butter
1 egg in cup, fill cup with milk

Mix all together till dough leaves the bowl clean. Cut dough in four pieces then cut each fourth into four, making sixteen scones.

Bake at 450°F for fifteen minutes.

P.S. May take a little more milk. Handle as little as possible.

73 LOTTIE LEE DAY'S TWICE COOKED MACAROONS

2 eggs whites
pinch of salt
1 cup sugar
1 1/2 teaspoons cornstarch
1 1/2 cups coconut
1/2 teaspoon vanilla
1/2 teaspoon almond flavoring

Beat egg whites with salt until stiff. Mix sugar with cornstarch. Gradually add sugar mixture to egg whites, beating until firm. Place in double boiler and cook over boiling water stirring constantly until crust forms on pan.

Add coconut and flavorings.

Prepare cookie sheets by greasing generously and coating thickly (about 1/8 inch) with mixture of 1/2 cornstarch and 1/2 icing sugar.

Drop mixture from a teaspoon on prepared pans.

Bake 30 minutes at 275°F until very lightly browned.

When cool store in tightly sealed container.

Makes about 3 dozen.

BUTTERSCOTCH REFRIGERATOR COOKIES 74

1 cup butter
2 cups brown sugar
2 eggs
1 teaspoon vanilla
3 cups flour
1/2 teaspoon salt
1 teaspoon soda
1 teaspoon cream of tartar

Cream butter and sugar. Add well beaten eggs and vanilla. Sift dry ingredients and then add gradually to the first mixture. Shape into 5 rolls approximately 1 3/4" x 7" long. Wrap in wax paper and place in refrigerator overnight. Slice very thin and bake on a greased cookie sheet at 400ºF for 8 minutes.

Variation:
Add 1 cup chopped walnuts. These can be rolled in foil and frozen unbaked. Ten minutes at room temperature and they're ready to slice.

DATE-FILLED OATMEAL COOKIES 75

2 cups oatmeal
2 cups flour
1/2 teaspoon salt
1 cup brown sugar, packed
1 cup shortening, lard or butter
1 teaspoon soda
1/2 cup sour milk

Mix dry ingredients. Cut in shortening. Mix soda with sour milk and stir in. Pat dough in a ball and chill thoroughly. Using 1/4 dough at a time roll out very thin and cut in circles 2" in diameter. Place on greased cookie sheet and bake 375ºF until crisp.

Date Filling:
Boil 1 cup chopped dates with 1/2 cup water and 1 tablespoon brown sugar, stirring until it becomes mushy and thick. Store in a jar and fill cookies just before serving — if you fill them too far ahead they may become soggy.

76   HOKEY POKEY COOKIES

Yields: 42

1/2 cup butter
1 cup sugar
1/2 teaspoon vanilla
1 Tablespoon golden syrup
2 Tablespoons milk
1 teaspoon soda
1 cup flour
pinch of salt
1 teaspoon baking powder

Cream butter, sugar and vanilla. Warm syrup and milk in small saucepan. Add soda and stir to dissolve. Add to first mixture. Blend in flour. Drop by teaspoon onto greased cookie sheets. Bake 200ºF for 1 hour — until cookies are crisp and golden.

Simple ingredients but amazing flavor — like seafoam candy. It must be the long slow cooking.

77   1933 GINGER SNAPS

4 cups flour
1 Tablespoon soda
1 Tablespoon ginger
pinch of salt
1/2 cup sugar
3/4 cup shortening
1 egg, beaten
1 cup molasses
1 Tablespoon vinegar
2 Tablespoons cold water

Sift dry ingredients together.

Cream sugar and shortening; add the egg, molasses, vinegar and water. Add dry ingredients. Roll on floured board to desired thickness and cut into shapes. Bake at 350ºF — 10 minutes.

This makes super gingerbread men.

SUGAR COOKIES

1 cup butter
1 cup sugar
2 eggs
1 teaspoon vanilla
2 teaspoons baking powder
2 1/2 cups flour

Cream butter and sugar.

Add eggs and vanilla and mix until fluffy.

Add dry ingredients.

Roll out on lightly floured board.

Cut into shapes as desired and sprinkle with sugar.

Bake at 350ºF for ten minutes or until very slightly brown. (Do not roll too thick or bake too long.)

This is it! THE recipe for Christmas cookie donkeys, stars and Santa Clauses.

If desired, omit sprinkling with sugar and paint with colored frosting — sprinkle with colored candies or chocolate shot.

SNICKERDOODLES

1 cup soft shortening
1 1/2 cups sugar
2 eggs, beaten
2 3/4 cups sifted flour
2 teaspoons cream of tartar
1 teaspoon soda
1/2 teaspoon salt

Cream shortening and sugar. Add beaten eggs.

Sift together dry ingredients. Add to first mixture.

Chill dough. Shape in small balls.

Roll in mixture of sugar and cinnamon.

Bake on lightly greased cookie sheets at 375ºF until lightly browned but still soft.

BOILED RAISIN SPICE CAKE

1 cup raisins
3 cups water
1 teaspoon soda
1 3/4 cups flour
1 teaspoon cinnamon
1/2 teaspoon nutmeg
1/2 teaspoon allspice
1/2 cup butter or margarine
1 cup dark brown sugar, firmly packed
1 egg
pinch of salt

Boil raisins in 3 cups of water, until 1 cup of liquid remains. Add 1 teaspoon soda, then drain raisins reserving the 1 cup of liquid. Sift together flour, cinnamon, allspice and nutmeg. Set aside. Cream butter until fluffy, gradually adding the brown sugar. Beat well, add egg and salt, beat until combined. Add some of hot raisin water to the butter mixture, alternately with the sifted flour and spices, stirring after each addition, until all is used. Stir in raisins last. Pour into greased and floured 9" x 9" pan. Bake at 350°F for 35-45 minutes. Ice when cool with Brown Sugar Icing.

Brown Sugar Icing:
1/3 cup butter
2/3 cup brown sugar, packed
3 Tablespoons milk
1 to 1 1/2 cups sifted icing sugar

Melt butter in saucepan. Add brown sugar and boil over low heat for two minutes, stirring constantly. Stir in milk and heat until mixture comes to a boil. Remove from heat and cool a bit. Gradually stir in sifted icing sugar. Spread over cool cake.

2 1/2 cups sifted cake flour
1 1/2 cups butter, softened
    (unsalted butter if possible)
2 1/4 cups firmly packed dark brown sugar
6 eggs
5 teaspoons vanilla
1 1/2 teaspoons lemon juice
icing sugar

Butter and lightly flour a 10" x 4" angel cake tube pan.

Sift flour onto wax paper.

Beat butter in large bowl (use electric mixer if you have one) until creamy and fluffy. Add brown sugar gradually beating well after each addition. Beat in eggs, one at at time, and continue to beat until mixture is light and fluffy, about five minutes. Beat in vanilla and lemon juice. Turn mixer to low speed and gradually blend in flour. Pour batter into prepared pan and level with spatula.

Bake in slow oven (325°F) for one hour and 20 minutes or until top springs back when lightly touched. Cool in pan on wire rack, for 20 minutes. Loosen around side and center tube with knife; remove from pan. Cool completely.

Lightly dust top with icing sugar before serving.

The dark brown sugar imparts a rich caramel flavor to this cake.

CANDY SQUARES   82

Make when the humidity is low
            1 cup brown sugar
            1 cup golden syrup
            1 cup cream
            1 teaspoon vanilla
            4 cups cornflakes
            1 cup salted peanuts
            2 cups Rice Krispies
            1 cup coconut

Cook sugar, syrup and cream to soft ball stage (as for fudge). Add vanilla. Pour over combined dry ingredients. Pat into 9" x 13" buttered pan.

CRUMB CAKE — OLD RECIPE — NEW WAY

In food processor or mix:

      2 cups flour
      1 cup sugar
      3/4 cup butter

Cut butter into 4 pieces, add to sugar and flour. Process in on-off bursts, scraping sides of container once or twice. Reserve 1 cup of this crumb mixture.

      Mix: remaining crumb mixture with
      1 teaspoon soda
      1/4 teaspoon salt
      1 teaspoon cloves
      1 teaspoon cinnamon
      1 cup sour milk
      1 egg

Process until well mixed.

Add: 1 cup raisins.

Buzz for 5 seconds.

Pour batter into greased and floured 9" pan.

Bake 350°F until just done, about 35-40 minutes.

Sprinkle reserved crumbs on top.

Bake an extra 5-8 minutes until crumbs are slightly golden.

1 pound butter
2 1/2 cups dark brown sugar, well packed
10 large eggs
1 1/2 pounds seeded raisins
1 pound seedless raisins
1/2 pound figs, chopped
1 pound dates, chopped
1 pound currants
1 pound candied cherries
1 pound mixed peel
1/2 pound sliced blanched almonds
1 large apple, finely chopped
3 1/2 cups flour
2 teaspoons baking soda
1 teaspoon salt
2 teaspoons cinnamon
1 teaspoon cloves
1 teaspoon vanilla
2 teaspoons brown vinegar
1/4 cup molasses
1 — 6 ounce glass crabapple jelly
juice of 1 lemon
2 Tablespoons cream

Sift and mix dry ingredients. Combine fruits and nuts with some of the measured flour.

Cream butter, add sugar and beat well. Add eggs one at a time and beat well. Should the mixture curdle add a little flour, then continue beating in remaining eggs. Add all other liquid ingredients alternating with dry ingredients. Then add the fruits and nuts, mixing thoroughly.

Cake pans should be lined, bottom and sides with a double layer of brown paper well greased. Fill pans 2/3 full, packing firmly with hands. Bake in a slow oven 200ºF-250ºF on middle oven rack. Will make 2 cakes, 8" x 8" x 2" and one loaf size. (Place coffee can of water in back of oven).

Note: When using 8" x 8" x 2" pyrex pans bake this cake for approximately 2 1/2 hours — longer if baked in deeper pans or pans of other dimensions.

Isn't there always left over Christmas cake? — This is great to take to the cottage — serve with sharp Cheddar cheese and cold lemonade.

BRIAN'S BIRTHDAY TORTE

1/2 cup butter or margarine
1 cup sugar
4 egg yolks, beaten
2 2/3 cups flour
5 teaspoons baking powder
1/2 teaspoon salt
1 cup milk
1 teaspoon vanilla
4 egg whites, beaten stiff
1 cup sugar

Cream butter until light, gradually add sugar. Beat in egg yolks. Sift flour, baking powder and salt and add to first mixture alternately with the milk — ending with flour mixture. Add vanilla. Beat egg whites to soft peak stage, gradually add sugar and beat until stiff. Add to batter, folding in gently. Pour batter into 3 buttered, floured 9" layer cake pans.

Bake 350ºF for approximately 20 minutes, or until done.

Cook cakes on racks. When cool, cut each layer in half horizontally. Layers may be frozen for easier cutting.

Spread Mocha Icing between layers and on top and sides.

Cover sides with toasted *ground* almonds and top with *toasted* slivered almonds.

Mocha Icing:
1 cup butter
4 cups icing sugar
4 egg yolks
1/4 cup heavy cream
1/4 teaspoon vanilla
1/4 cup TRIPLE strength coffee*
*make coffee using 6 Tablespoons instant
    coffee and 1/4 cup hot water.

Cream butter until light and fluffy.

Add icing sugar gradually.

Add egg yolks one at a time, beating well after each addition.

Add liquids.

Be sure cake is cooled before handling, as layers are quite thin. Layers may be made ahead of time and frozen for easier cutting and handling.

GATEAU DE NOEL (BELGIAN FRUIT CAKE)

1 pound butter (no substitutes)
2 cups sugar
9 eggs
5 cups flour
1 pound candied peel
1/2 pound light raisins
1/2 pound chopped almonds

Cream butter and sugar together for 15 minutes by hand, or 8-10 minutes with mixer. Continue beating, add the eggs, 2 at a time.

Fold in flour, peel and nuts.

Grease large loaf pan (12" x 5" x 3") and line with double layers of greased brown paper — sides and bottom.

Pack fruit cake into pan.

Bake 325°F until done, approximately two hours.

RHUBARB CRUMBLE PIE

1/2 cup melted butter
1/2 cup flour
1 1/2 cups rolled oats
2/3 cup brown sugar, packed
3 cups cut rhubarb
1 1/2 Tablespoons flour
1/2 cup sugar
1 egg beaten

Combine first four ingredients. Using 3/4 of the mixture, pat firmly on bottom of buttered 9" pie plate.

Combine rhubarb, flour, sugar and beaten egg. Pour over oatmeal base. Sprinkle with rest of oatmeal mixture.

Bake 350°F 40-45 minutes.

Serve with thick farm cream or sweetened whipped cream.

88   APPLE DUMPLINGS

Serves 6

Pastry:

1 1/2 cups flour
2 teaspoons baking powder
1/2 teaspoon salt
2 Tablespoons lard or shortening
2 Tablespoons butter
1/2 cup water

Sift dry ingredients, cut in butter and lard. Blend in water. Pat dough out onto floured surface and roll to 1 inch thickness and cover with apple mixture. Roll as for jelly roll. Bake in oven-proof dish with 1/2 cup of sauce.

Filling:

2 cups chopped apple
1/2 cup brown sugar
1/2 teaspoon nutmeg
1/2 teaspoon cinnamon

Sauce:

2 cups sugar
2 Tablespoons flour
2 cups water
4 Tablespoons butter
2 teaspoons vanilla

Mix and cook over low to medium heat until thick. Add vanilla. Use remaining hot sauce to pour a little over each serving.

89   LEMON PUDDING

Serves 6

1 cup sugar
1 Tablespoon butter
3 level Tablespoons flour
juice and grated rind of 1 lemon
2 eggs, separated
1 cup milk
1/4 teaspoon salt

Cream butter and sugar until light and fluffy. Add lemon rind and flour, then beaten egg yolks, milk and lemon juice.

Fold in stiffly beaten egg whites and salt. Pour into buttered souffle dish. Place dish in pan of boiling water, so that water comes 1/2 way up sides of souffle dish.

Bake 300ºF 45 minutes-1 hour.

FRUIT IN SATIN

Serves
8-10

3 egg yolks
2 Tablespoons sugar
3 Tablespoons vinegar
2 Tablespoons pineapple syrup
2 Tablespoons butter
1/4 teaspoon salt

Mix well, then cook in double boiler until thickened. Stir continuously. Allow to cool.

Add:

2 oranges (peeled and cut into sections)
1 cup peaches*, sliced
1 cup maraschino cherries (drained)
1 cup canned pineapple (drained)
1 cup seedless grapes
12 marshmallows, cut up

Mix with cooled sauce.

Note: Canned fruits, drained, may be used when fresh is not available.

Whip 1 cup cream — fold into fruit mixture — refrigerate at least 6 hours. Serve in glass bowl — top with sweetened whipped cream, garnish with toasted almonds and more green grapes or fresh strawberries.

LEMON CURD

6 eggs
2 egg yolks
2 cups sugar
1/4 cup grated lemon peel
3/4 cup fresh lemon juice
1 cup butter

In top of double boiler, combine eggs, egg yolks and sugar. Mix well.

Add lemon peel, lemon juice and butter. Cook gently over boiling water, stirring frequently until mixture is smooth and quite thick.

Remove from heat and cool.

To store: Turn into glass jars or plastic containers. Will keep well in refrigerator. Also freezes beautifully.

The definitive lemon tart filling.

8 inch sponge cake
coconut macaroons
1/2 cup sherry
1 cup jam — raspberry or apricot
3 cups thin custard sauce
1 can pineapple tidbits, drained
4 or 5 medium bananas
1/2 cup toasted slivered almonds
2 oranges, sectioned, chopped
1/2 pint whipping cream

Break up sponge cake into bite size pieces and toss into bottom of large glass bowl. Do the same with the macaroons. Pour some sherry over, until just soaked up. Drop half the jam in small gobs on top and then pour about half the custard over. The next layer consists of all the bananas sliced and tossed in, then the orange bits and the pineapple tidbits, then the rest of the sherry, daubs of the remaining jam, toasted almonds and remaining custard. Poke a few red cherries in anywhere so they may be seen through the glass bowl. Whip cream and spread on top.

Refrigerate for 4-5 hours before serving.

Macaroons:
1/2 cup sweetened condensed milk
2 cups coconut
1 teaspoon almond flavoring

Mix well. Drop by teaspoon onto well oiled cookie sheet. Bake at 350ºF for ten minutes or until firm and slightly colored. Remove immediately from pan. If you double the recipe it allows a few extra to eat!

Custard Sauce:
3 1/4 cups milk (homogenized)
1/3 cup sugar
2 egg yolks, beaten
2 Tablespoons cornstarch
1/4 teaspoon salt
1 teaspoon vanilla

Mix cornstarch and sugar. In heavy saucepan combine all ingredients except vanilla. Cook over low to medium heat, stirring constantly with wire whisk or spoon (10 to 15 minutes) until mixture coats a spoon. Remove from heat, add vanilla, cover and chill.

(continued)

The sauce thickens slightly as it cools. If too thick, more milk may be whisked in.

Shortcut for custard sauce is to use one package Banana Cream Pie Filling, following directions on package but using *three* cups milk instead of two.

Variations: Instead of a sponge cake, 1/2 inch slices of jelly roll (you can buy this) look lovely arranged so as to be seen through the glass bowl. Make sure it absorbs some of the custard and sherry.

MOCHA ANGEL PIE   93

3 egg whites at room temperature
1/4 teaspoon cream of tartar
dash of salt
3/4 cup berry sugar

Beat egg whites until stiff; add cream of tartar and salt. Very slowly, while still beating, add sugar a spoonful at a time. Beat until very stiff and meringue feels smooth when rubbed between fingers. Spread over bottom and well up on sides of buttered 8" pie plate. Bake 275°F for 1 hour.

Filling:
2 cups semi-sweet chocolate chips
1 Tablespoon instant coffee
1/4 cup boiling water
1/4 cup light corn syrup
3 egg yolks
1 cup heavy cream, whipped
1 teaspoon vanilla

Melt chocolate over hot (not boiling) water.

Combine coffee, boiling water and syrup, beat in egg yolks.

Stir in melted chocolate — cool several minutes, stirring now and then.

Fold in whipped cream with vanilla.

Pour into baked shell and chill.

94 BAKED BANANAS

8 firm bananas, each cut in three
1/2 cup melted butter

Roll bananas in butter and bake five minutes at 350°F in 9" x 13" pyrex dish.

Mix:
1/2 cup brown sugar
2 Tablespoons cornstarch
2 Tablespoons orange rind
pinch cloves
1 1/2 cups orange juice

Cook above mixture until thickened and pour over bananas. This may all be done ahead. When almost ready to serve, bake 10 minutes at 350°F and serve hot with rum sauce and ice cream if desired.

Rum Sauce:
2 egg yolks
1/2 cup icing sugar
1/2 cup cream
pinch salt
2 ounces rum
2 beaten egg whites

Combine first four ingredients.

Beat over medium heat until thick. Cool. Add 2 ounces rum. Refrigerate. This much can be done ahead. Before serving, beat egg whites until stiff and fold in.

MRS. MURRAY'S POPCORN BALLS

25 to 30 cups salted popped popcorn in one or more very large bowls.

    1 cup sugar
    1 cup molasses
    2 Tablespoons vinegar
    4 Tablespoons butter
    1 cup cold water
    1/2 teaspoon baking soda

Mix sugar, molasses, vinegar, butter and water in heavy saucepan. Boil to hard ball stage. Then add baking soda. Watch it doesn't boil over.

Pour over popcorn and mix well.

Run hands under cold water, shake off excess. Form popcorn balls. When cool and set, wrap in plastic wrap.

BURNT SUGAR FUDGE

    3 cups sugar
    1 cup milk
    few grains salt
    1 cup sugar
    1 cup chopped walnuts
    1 teaspoon vanilla

Combine 3 cups sugar, milk and salt and cook to soft ball stage on top of stove. Set aside. Put into frying pan remaining 1 cup of sugar. Using long wooden spoon stir over high heat until sugar melts and turns brown. Pour this into the fudge. Add walnuts and vanilla. Beat until creamy and beginning to stiffen. Pour into buttered 8" x 8" square pan. When completely cooled and firm, cut into squares.

97 OLD IRISH MARMALADE

Yields:
8-1/2pints

3 pounds *Seville* oranges
2 large lemons
7 pounds sugar

Wash, then squeeze fruit (Save pips — put in a cup and cover with water).

Slice or mince rinds in food processor or large blade food chopper. Put in a bowl, cover with 2 quarts cold water. Let stand 24 hours. Drain pips, reserving thick liquid. Tie "pips" in gauze, boil with rinds, juices and pip liquid for 1/2 hour. Add sugar and boil 1 1/2 to 2 hours. Remove bag of "pips". Start testing for jelly stage — 225°F on jelly thermometer. When jelly stage is reached pour into hot sterilized jars, covering with paraffin. Makes superb, dark, bitter marmalade.

98 MY GRANDMOTHER'S CHUTNEY

Yields:
5 pints

12 sour apples
1 large onion
2 green peppers
1 red pepper
1 cup raisins
1 pint vinegar
6 plums
6 peaches
3 cups sugar
4 lemons (juice)
1 teaspoon ginger
1/4 teaspoon cayenne
1 teaspoon salt

Chop fruit, onion and peppers.

Add vinegar. Simmer one hour.

Then add other ingredients and simmer another hour, stirring frequently.

Bottle in hot sterilized jars and seal tightly.

2 large cauliflowers, separated into flowerets
4 pounds pickling cucumbers, in chunks
8 pounds small white pickling onions, skinned
2 or 3 red peppers, in strips or chunks
2 or 3 green peppers, in strips or chunks

Brine:
4 quarts water
1 pint pickling salt (not iodized)

Pour brine over prepared vegetables and leave overnight, stirring occasionally. Pour off brine. Taste vegetables for saltiness. If too salty, rinse in cold water.

Mustard Sauce:
2 quarts white vinegar
3 cups sugar
1 cup flour
6 Tablespoons Keen's dry mustard
1 Tablespoon turmeric
1 quart white vinegar

Heat 2 quarts white vinegar with sugar

Mix flour, mustard, turmeric. Add 1 quart vinegar to make a smooth paste. Add to hot vinegar-sugar mixture.

Cook without boiling in a large heavy kettle until slightly thickened, stirring often. Add drained vegetables and heat until thoroughly hot but not boiling. Pour immediately into hot sterilized sealers. Seal tightly.

Flavors need time to blend. Open the first jar for Thanksgiving dinner.

100   CALICO MUSTARD RELISH

Yields:
12 jars

4 large cucumbers
1 large cauliflower, or 2 small
10 medium size onions
6 red sweet peppers
1 big bunch celery (cut off tops)

Grind the above ingredients in chopper or grinder. Place in large china bowl, sprinkle with salt and let stand overnight at room temperature.

6 cups cider vinegar
8 cups white sugar
2 ounces mustard seed
1/2 ounce celery seed
1 1/4 cups flour
1 teaspoon dry mustard
1/2 ounce turmeric powder

Next day, drain vegetables, and rinse with cold water. Drain well. Heat vinegar and sugar, add mustard seed, and celery seed. Make a paste with dry mustard, turmeric and flour, and some of the vinegar. Add to the vinegar mixture, stirring until thick and smooth. Add vegetables and stir. Let stand one hour on very low heat. Do not boil, just keep very hot. Stir occasionally, to keep from sticking. Pour into hot sterilized jars and cover with melted paraffin.

101   GREEN TOMATO PICKLE

5 pounds green tomatoes, sliced
2 1/2 pounds onions, sliced
1/4 cup pickling salt

Mix. Leave overnight in large bowl, then drain.

The Next Day:
Mix:

3 cups sugar
2 1/2 cups white vinegar
1/2 cup water
1/4 cup mixed pickling spices,
    tied in a bag

Bring mixture to a boil. Add tomatoes and onions. Cook 1 1/2 hours.

Stir in 1 teaspoon mustard and 1/2 teaspoon cayenne pepper. Pour into hot, sterilized jars. Seal tightly.

Midweek Gourmet

Top picture:	(clockwise from the top)
	Fresh Tomato Soup
	Pasta With Prezzemolo Sauce
	Papaya Salad

Bottom picture:	(from left to right)
	Grapes in Brandy
	Blender Pecan Torte

CHICKEN SOUP MIKADO

Serves 8

8 green onions
2 chicken breasts, cut into 1" pieces
10 cups chicken broth, homemade or canned
1 Tablespoon soya sauce
4 Tablespoons sake
freshly grated ginger

Cut white part of onions into 2" lengthwise strips and soak in cold water for several hours.

Bring to boil the broth and add chicken pieces. Simmer gently until chicken is cooked but not tough.

Before serving, add soya sauce and sake.

Drain onion strips, squeezing juice of ginger over onion.

Divide onions among 8 bowls and fill bowls with soup.

Garnish with thin carrot slices cut to resemble flowers.

CREME BORDELAISE

Serves 8

1 pound frozen green peas
1 can chicken consomme or homemade stock
1 teaspoon sugar
1 Tablespoon butter
4 green onions, chopped
2 Tablespoons flour
2 Tablespoons fresh mint
2 cups milk or cream
salt
pepper

Mix first 5 ingredients together and cook for 20-30 minutes. Put in food processor with fresh mint. Add milk or cream. Season with salt and pepper. Buzz to make a smooth mixture. If too thick, add more milk. Garnish with pieces of lime. Serve hot or cold.

104 GRANDMOTHER'S CLAM CHOWDER

Serves 8

2 — 5.2 ounce cans baby clams
12 slices bacon, chopped
2 medium onions, grated
2 Tablespoons butter
1/2 teaspoon salt
1/4 teaspoon pepper
2 large cans evaporated milk
4 medium raw potatoes peeled and grated

Saute onion in butter in skillet or fry pan until transparent (not brown). Remove onions to large pot. Saute chopped bacon in skillet. Remove bacon with slotted spoon and add to onions. Add grated potato. Cover with water and simmer until cooked. Add clams (not drained) and milk. Simmer until heated through. *Do not boil.* Adjust seasonings. A few drops of pepper sauce (i.e. Tabasco) may be added for extra zip if desired.

105 FISH CHOWDER

Serves 6

1 pound haddock
1 can clams and juice
1 can clam chowder soup
   (New England Style)
1 regular can Carnation evaporated milk

Cook haddock in water gently until tender and flakes easily. Heat clams, juice, chowder and milk. Add flaked haddock.

Serve piping hot with a knob of butter and a sprig of parsley.

Serves 8

1 cup sliced fresh mushrooms
4 Tablespoons butter
2 cans cream of mushroom soup
1 can rich chicken stock, or more

Saute mushrooms in butter until the mushroom liquid evaporates. Mix mushroom soup with chicken stock and heat. Add mushrooms. Serve immediately, garnished with sprigs of watercress.

Note: The mushrooms will render up some juice. Enough stock should be added to give a thick rich soup — do not make it thin.

FRESH TOMATO SOUP 107

8 cups water
1 Tablespoon salt
1/4 teaspoon pepper
2 Tablespoons butter
2 onions, chopped
4 unpeeled tomatoes, quartered
1 teaspoon sugar
4 potatoes, peeled and diced
1/2 cup rich cream

Bring water to a boil in a soup pot, adding salt and pepper. Melt butter in frying pan and saute onion gently. When onion is golden and a little brown add tomatoes and stir until covered with butter. Add this mixture to boiling water in soup kettle. Add sugar and potatoes. Cover and simmer for 1 hour. Press soup through a sieve, add rich cream, stirring quickly so that soup will not curdle. Reheat but do not boil. Taste for seasoning.

108 CREAM CHEESE ENTREE (A COLD SOUP)

Serves 6

1 — 8 ounce package Philadelphia cream cheese
1 — 10 ounce can consomme
1 teaspoon curry powder

Place cream cheese and curry powder in blender. Add 3/4 can consomme, reserving remainder. Blend at high speed until smooth.

Pour into small individual dishes and refrigerate until firm. Warm remaining consomme until smooth, cool and pour over tops to form glaze.

Garnish with sprigs of watercress.

Note: Winnipeg cream cheese, which is a whipped variety, also works well.

109 ZUCCHINI SOUP

Serves 8-10

1 large onion, chopped
2 Tablespoons butter or margarine
2 chicken bouillon cubes or
    2 Tablespoons chicken essence
2 cups boiling water
4 cups cubed zucchini (remove seeds if large)
1/2 teaspoon salt
1/8 teaspoon garlic powder
1/8 teaspoon celery salt
dash pepper
1/4 cup parsley leaves

Combine all but parsley and simmer 5 minutes until tender. Puree after adding parsley. May be served with Jalapeno pepper cheese, cubed, on top.

Freezes well.

This is a great soup and one of the easiest. Can't find Jalapeno cheese? Use a dab of sour cream and a dot of Jalapeno jelly on top.

PAPAYA SALAD

Serves 10

1 medium mild onion, sliced in rings
4 papayas
4 oranges
8 ripe olives, sliced
    OR pomegranate seeds
1 cup undiluted frozen orange juice
6 Tablespoons good olive oil
salt
freshly ground black pepper

Peel, seed and slice papaya lengthwise in large pieces. Peel oranges and slice crosswise in "wheels". Add sliced black olives or pomegranate seeds. Blend orange juice well with olive oil, add generous amounts of salt and coarsely ground pepper.

Refrigerate, covered until serving time.

When ready to serve, drain and serve on a bed of romaine or curly endive. Will keep overnight.

CANTALOUPE AND BLACKBERRY SALAD

4 cantaloupes
4 cups fresh or frozen blackberries

Peel and seed cantaloupes and cut into balls. Mix with blackberries. Serve with lime and honey dressing in butter lettuce cups.

Lime and Honey Dressing
1 cup salad oil
1/3 cup honey
1/2 cup lime juice
1/4 teaspoon mild mustard
paprika
salt
2 grated lime rinds

In blender combine all ingredients. Blend well. Chill.

112 ASPARAGUS VINAIGRETTE

Serves 4

1 pound fresh asparagus
1/2 cup water
2 teaspoons Beau Monde Seasoning
1/2 teaspoon cracked black pepper
1/4 teaspoon mild prepared mustard
5 Tablespoons olive oil
2 Tablespoons white wine vinegar
1 Tablespoon sour cream
1 hard cooked egg, finely chopped
1 teaspoon chopped parsley

Trim and wash asparagus and scrape off scales. Cover asparagus with water. Add 1 teaspoon of Beau Monde Seasoning. Do not cover pan. Cook until barely tender. Meanwhile, combine in a bowl 1 teaspoon Beau Monde, pepper, mustard, vinegar, oil and sour cream. Beat well. Stir in finely chopped egg and parsley. Drain asparagus well and cover with sauce. Reheat thoroughly and serve at once.

113 CHAMPIGNONS À LA CRÉME

Serves 4

4 slices ham, chopped
1 pound mushrooms
4 Tablespoons unsalted butter
1/4 teaspoon salt
1/4 teaspoon black pepper
1/2 teaspoon dried mixed herbs
    (thyme, sage, bay leaf, coriander,
    mace)
1 Tablespoon flour
1/2 cup heavy cream
1 Tablespoon chopped parsley
juice of one-half lemon

Melt butter in saucepan and saute mushrooms. Season to taste with salt, pepper and mixed herbs.

Add chopped ham and toss. Cook for a few minutes.

Sprinkle flour over and stir. Gradually stir in cream, stirring constantly. Simmer, do not boil.

Add parsley and lemon juice.

Serve on fried French bread.

CELERY CASSEROLE   114

Serves 8

4 cups celery, sliced
1 can Chinese water chestnuts, sliced
1/4 cup chopped pimento
1/3 cup sliced almonds
1/4 cup bread crumbs
1 can cream of chicken soup
salt
pepper

Parboil celery, drain, reserving 1/4 cup of water. Blend water with soup, pimento, salt and pepper and bread crumbs. Layer celery, water chestnuts and almonds (save a few almonds for garnish) in casserole dish. Pour soup mixture over and sprinkle with reserved almonds.

Bake in uncovered casserole for 45 minutes at 325°F.

Serve hot.

PANNED POTATOES   115

8-10 small peeled whole potatoes
1/2 cup butter
salt

Melt butter in electric frying pan. Add potatoes, salt well, rolling potatoes around to coat with butter. Set frying pan heat at 240°F. Cover pan, making sure vent is closed. Bake 40-50 minutes or until potatoes are done. This will depend on size and age of potato.

During cooking, turn potatoes three or four times to brown all over.

These have a particularly nice flavor.

116 OVEN BAKED FRENCH TOAST BRUNCH SPECIAL

Serves
4-6

1/4 cup butter
2 Tablespoons liquid honey
1/2 teaspoon cinnamon
3 eggs, beaten
1/2 cup fresh orange juice
1/8 teaspoon salt
6 slices fine whole wheat bread

Melt butter and honey in a 9" x 13" pan. Mix well. Sprinkle cinnamon over that mixture. Beat eggs, juice and salt together. Quickly soak bread slices in mixture. Arrange slices in pan. Bake in preheated 400ºF oven for 20 minutes or until set and golden brown. Invert toast for serving.

This can be made for hoards of hungry kids — It's sweet enough to be a snack after a team practice.

117 BAKED HAM OMELET

Serves
6-8

1 pound Monterey Jack cheese
2 cups cubed ham
salt
pepper
Tabasco sauce
1 dozen eggs
1/2 cup sifted flour
1 teaspoon baking powder
1/2 cup melted butter
1 pint small curd or creamed
    cottage cheese

Preheat oven to 400ºF.

Shred cheese, cube ham.

Beat eggs and season lightly with salt and pepper. Add 5-6 drops of Tabasco sauce. Stir in flour, baking powder, ham, cheese, cottage cheese and half of melted butter.

Pour other half of melted butter into 9" x 13" baking dish to coat evenly.

Pour in egg mixture. Bake at 400ºF for 15 minutes.

Reduce heat to 350ºF and bake for 20-25 minutes or until light brown on top.

STUFFED GREEN PEPPERS 118

3 or 4 green peppers
1 pound lean ground beef
1/2 pound bread crumbs
2 eggs
2 heaping Tablespoons of freshly grated
    Parmesan cheese
1 garlic clove, chopped
1 Tablespoon tomato sauce per
    pepper half
pinch of salt
pinch of black pepper
more tomato sauce

Place meat and chopped garlic in frying pan and cook until brown. Drain excess fat from meat and put meat in large mixing bowl. Add bread crumbs, cheese, salt, pepper, eggs and tomato sauce. Mix thoroughly.

Wash peppers and cut in half through the stem, remove the seeds and stuff halves with the mixture. Lightly cover the bottom of casserole dish with tomato sauce and place stuffed peppers in dish. Put some tomato sauce on the top of the stuffed peppers and sprinkle lightly with Parmesan cheese. Bake in 350ºF oven for 30 minutes or until the peppers are cooked but still retain their shape.

Tomato Sauce
1/4 small onion, chopped fine
1 garlic clove, chopped fine
1 — 16 ounce can of plum tomatoes
3 Tablespoons cooking oil
pinch of sweet basil
pinch of salt
pinch of pepper

Place cooking oil into deep saucepan and brown garlic and onion. Mix in tomatoes and spices and cook over moderate heat until tomatoes break down, stirring occasionally. Simmer 15 minutes or until sauce thickens a little.

ALBERTA WILD DUCKS

Serves 6-8

5 ducks, cleaned and dried
3 red apples, cored and quartered
1 cup Burgundy wine
1/2 cup water

The night before serving stuff ducks with apples. Place in large roasting pan. Pour wine and water over ducks. Cover pan and bake in a 325°F oven for 2 hours, or until very tender. Pour off juice and chill the ducks till they are cold enough to allow the meat to slice easily. Carve ducks into slices, and store in refrigerator until 1 hour before you plan to serve them. Meanwhile, make the following sauce:

1 cup butter
1/3 cup lemon juice
1/4 cup chopped parsley
1 Tablespoon Worcestershire sauce
1/4 cup chopped green onions with tops
1 1/2 teaspoons prepared mustard
salt
pepper

Melt butter in heavy saucepan and stir in half the lemon juice. Heat until very hot but not boiling. Taste sauce which should be tart but not sour, add more lemon juice if needed. Add parsley, Worcestershire sauce, onions, mustard and stir well.

To assemble put one-quarter of duck meat in casserole. Season with salt and pepper, drizzle with lemon butter sauce and continue until all duck and sauce are used. Cover and bake in a 325°F oven for one hour.

Serve with Fried Rice.

FRIED RICE

Serves 8

3 cups cold cooked rice (white)
soya sauce
1 cup chopped cooked ham or bacon
1 can mushroom pieces
1 jar pimento, cut in strips
1 green pepper, cut in strips
2-3 green onions, chopped
1 can water chestnuts, drained and sliced

Heat rice in hot vegetable oil using a large skillet.

Add enough soya sauce to turn the rice a light brown color. Stir.

Add other ingredients and heat thoroughly over medium heat 20-30 minutes, stirring occasionally to prevent the mixture from sticking.

Recipe may be doubled or tripled.

GROUSE IN GRAPE JUICE

1 grouse or fat mallard duck
1/4 cup butter
1 cup grape juice
1 cup port wine
1 clove
1 bay leaf
salt and pepper to season

Cut grouse in half and sprinkle with salt and pepper. Brown in butter and pour off excess fat. Mix grape juice with port wine. Add clove and bay leaf. Pour sauce over grouse. Cover and bake in a slow oven, 275°F for 2 hours, turning and basting frequently.

Try Papaya Salad with this.

122 SWEET AND SOUR CHICKEN BALLS

Serves 4

1 1/2 pounds boned chicken breasts
1 egg, slightly beaten
2/3 cup milk
1 Tablespoon oil
1 cup flour
1 1/2 teaspoons baking powder
1 1/2 teaspoons salt

Cut chicken in thin pieces about 2 inches long. Make batter by combining beaten egg with milk and oil. Sift together flour, baking powder and salt and add to egg mixture. Mix well. Dip chicken pieces in batter and deep-fry for 5-6 minutes at 350°F. Pour sweet and sour sauce over cooked chicken pieces just before serving. Serve with steamed or fried rice.

Sweet and Sour Sauce
1/2 cup sugar
1/2 cup vinegar
1/2 cup chicken broth
1 can pineapple chunks (not drained)
dash Tabasco
1/8 teaspoon salt
1 teaspoon cornstarch

In saucepan combine sugar, vinegar, chicken broth, Tabasco and salt and bring to boil. Mix cornstarch with the juice from the pineapple and stir into boiling sauce. Add pineapple. Stir until slightly thickened. Remove from heat and pour over chicken pieces.

123 MUSHROOMS IN PATTY SHELLS

small patty shells, cooked
1 pound mushrooms*
1/2 pound ground raw pork
1/4 cup minced water chestnuts
1/4 cup minced green onions
1 egg
1 teaspoon soya sauce
1/2 teaspoon salt

(continued)

pepper
melted butter
sesame seeds

*Mushrooms should be size to fit whole into patty shells. Reserve enough to top each patty shell. Chop remainder. In frying pan, brown pork, add water chestnuts, green onion, soya sauce, salt and pepper. When hot, quickly stir in egg. Remove from heat. Place filling in patty shells. Dip remaining whole mushrooms in a little melted butter — Top each patty shell with mushroom cap — Sprinkle with sesame seeds.

Bake 350°F for 35 minutes. May be used as an appetizer or a side dish with Chinese food.

CHINESE BEEF WITH VEGETABLES   124

Serves 8

1 pound tender beef (sirloin preferred)
2 Tablespoons cornstarch
2 Tablespoons soya sauce
2 Tablespoons dry white Vermouth
1 teaspoon sugar
4 cups chopped vegetables cut in
    uniform sizes
      e.g. green pepper, pimento strips,
        celery (with leaves), green onion
        (green part too), mushrooms,
        Chinese vegetables (water chestnuts,
        bok choy, etc., Chinese pea pods)
3 slices fresh ginger root, 1/8 inch thick
3 Tablespoons vegetable oil
    (more if necessary)
1 teaspoon salt
3/4 cup chicken stock

Slice beef in long narrow strips.

Combine next four ingredients and marinate beef for 20 minutes.

Heat oil in large wok. Stir fry beef quickly, a few pieces at a time — pieces must not touch or they will give up their juices. Remove beef to warm dish. Add more oil if ncessary. Add ginger root. Add vegetables and salt and stir fry. Stir in stock, heat quickly. Return beef to wok — heat through. Serve at once.

CHICKEN BREASTS IN LEMONY CREAM SAUCE

Serves 4

4 boned chicken breasts
5 Tablespoons butter
finely grated peel of 2 lemons
1 teaspoon minced garlic
8 large mushrooms sliced
3 Tablespoons flour
1/2 teaspoon salt
1/4 teaspoon white pepper
1 1/4 cups chicken stock (or same amount
    of water and 1 chicken cube)
1 cup sour cream
1 cup whipping cream
juice of 1 lemon
3 Tablespoons grated Parmesan cheese
    (optional)
2 Tablespoons finely chopped parsley

Preheat oven to 350°F.

In a frying pan heat 2 Tablespoons butter and brown chicken breasts, adding more butter if necessary.

Remove chicken breasts and keep warm.

In the same pan melt 3 Tablespoons of butter and add the lemon peel, garlic and mushrooms.

Cook for 2 minutes.

Remove from heat. Add the flour gradually and stir until it absorbs the butter.

Slowly add the chicken stock, salt and pepper and stir over low heat until the sauce is thickened.

Beat the whipping cream until thick and fold the sour cream into it.

Off the heat add the cream and lemon juice to the sauce.

Place the chicken breasts in an oven proof casserole and completely cover with the sauce.

Bake for 35 to 40 minutes.

The optional cheese may be sprinkled on top and browned under the broiler.

Decorate with parsley and serve.

Serves
8-10

1/3 cup flour
2 teaspoons salt
1/2 teaspoon pepper
2 pounds round steak, cubed
1/3 cup olive oil
2 cloves garlic, crushed
2 cans beef broth
2 cups Burgundy
1/2 teaspoon marjoram
1/2 teaspoon dried dill weed
3 cups fresh sliced mushrooms
2 packages (about 8) cooked artichoke hearts
1/3 cup flour
1/2 cup water
2 cans baking powder biscuits (sweetmilk)
    from dairy shelf or your own pastry

Mix flour, salt and pepper in bowl and dredge beef. In a large skillet, heat oil and garlic and brown beef. Do only a few at a time so that beef pieces do not touch each other. Return all cooked beef to pan, add beef broth, Burgundy, marjoram and dill weed. Cover and simmer 1 1/2 hours. Add artichoke hearts and mushrooms. Cook 10 minutes more. Mix flour and water to a paste and stir in mixture. Stir and cook until thickened. Place in 2 — 2 quart casseroles. Cover and place in fridge or freezer.

For Frozen Casserole: Heat in oven covered at 400ºF for 1 1/2 hours. Stir, then cook 30 minutes more. Top with biscuits or pastry and bake a further 12-15 minutes.

For Unfrozen Casserole: Top with biscuits or pastry and bake 400ºF for 12-15 minutes, a little longer for pastry.

127 PREZZEMOLO SAUCE — THE STRAWBERRY CAFE

A rich parsley sauce used like pesto.

> 4 bunches parsley (use leaves only)
> 2 1/2 cups rich olive oil
> 2 cloves garlic
> salt
> pepper
> 1/2 pound pine nuts

Buzz parsley leaves in food processor until very fine. Add garlic buds while motor is running. Add other ingredients and blend to a thick green sauce.

At this point you may freeze it. If using it now — add lots of Parmesan.

Prezzemolo Sauce is a marvellous Italian sauce — to be used in many ways. It keeps well in the refrigerator and the freezer. Freeze in ice cube containers — use one or two cubes as needed, adding fresh ground Parmesan at the last minute.

Try a little prezzemolo in vegetable soups, over freshly cooked vegetables (it does wonders for bland zucchini) as a basting sauce when barbecuing chicken, steaks and fish — and of course with pasta cooked al dente.

128 PASTA PREZZEMOLO

Serves
4-6

> 1 pound fusilli or pencil macaroni
> 1 Tablespoon butter
> fresh vegetables — broccoli,
>   asparagus tips, zucchini slices
> prezzemolo sauce (above)
> cherry tomatoes
> fresh parsley

Cook fusilli or pencil macaroni al dente. Drain, add butter and stir. Add a mixture of freshly steamed vegetables. Toss with some prezzemolo. Garnish with tomatoes and parsley. Serve immediately.

VEAL CUTLETS MARSALA   129

Serves 6-8

10 small veal cutlets (tender beef
    can be substituted)
1/2 cup flour.
1 teaspoon salt
1/2 teaspoon pepper
1/4 cup oil
1/2 cup Dry Marsala Wine
1/2 cup chicken stock

Mix flour, salt and pepper. Coat cutlets in flour mixture. Heat oil in skillet and saute cutlets until golden. Place meat on a warm serving platter. To skillet add broth and Marsala Wine, scraping bottom of pan. Pour liquid on top of cutlets. Serve at once. Serve with Rice Milanese with Cauliflower and Peas.

RICE MILANESE WITH   130
CAULIFLOWER AND PEAS

Serves 6-8

1/2 cup butter
1 onion, finely chopped
1/2 cup fresh mushrooms, sliced thinly
1/2 cup frozen peas
1 cup ham, finely shredded
2 cups long grain rice
1 teaspoon salt
1/2 teaspoon pepper
4 cups chicken broth
1/4 cup Dry Marsala Wine
1/8 teaspoon Saffron (optional)
1/2 cup freshly grated Parmesan cheese
1 head cauliflower, cut in florets
2 Tablespoons butter

Saute onion in butter until soft. Add mushrooms, peas and ham. Stir well about two minutes. Add rice and stir well with other ingredients. Season with salt and pepper. Add chicken broth and Marsala Wine. Cover and cook for 15 minutes or until rice is fluffy and tender. Add the Saffron, stirring well.

While rice is cooking, cook the cauliflower in a small amount of salted, boiling water. Drain. Stir in butter and arrange florets around the platter. Pour cooked rice into centre. Sprinkle all with Parmesan cheese. Serve immediately. Excellent with Veal Cutlets Marsala.

131   NASSI GORENG

Lunch or supper cooked in wok or frying pan.

Serves 4

2 Tablespoons oil
1 Tablespoon butter
3 slices bacon, diced
1 small onion, chopped
1-2 cloves garlic, crushed

In a wok or frying pan heat oil and butter. Saute bacon, onion and garlic.

Add:

1 Tablespoon chutney
1/2 teaspoon Sambal Oelek (optional)
2 teaspoons soya sauce
1 teaspoon coriander

Mix well and add:

1 leek, sliced
2 celery stalks, chopped

cook gently until almost done

Add:

3 cups cooked rice and mix well
1/2 pound cooked cubed chicken or lamb
1/2 cup chopped ham
1/4 pound small cooked shrimp

Heat through. Add salt and pepper to taste. Pile onto serving platter, garnish with strips of crepes and fried bananas.

132   OVEN FRIED TROUT

Dip cleaned whole trout in salted milk, then dredge in fine dry bread crumbs. Flour, corn meal or cracker crumbs do not produce satisfactory results. Place fish on oiled foil on jelly roll sheet and sprinkle with melted butter.

Measure trout at thickest part.

Bake in preheated oven — 425°F, 10 minutes per inch thickness.

Slide fish gently onto platter, foil too.

Garnish with lemon wedges and watercress.

Serve with skillet potatoes.

Serves 6

3 Tablespoons butter
6 boiled new potatoes
1 green onion (top too)
salt, pepper

Heat butter in heavy skillet, add finely minced green onion. Grate potatoes (they handle best when cold), add salt and pepper. Pack potatoes down.

Cook slowly, without stirring until underside of potatoes is brown and crisp. Then, beginning on one side, slowly fold potatoes over, as you would on omelet. Turn out onto a heated platter and serve at once.

TRIPLE DECK LOAF —   **134**
HAM-VEAL-MUSHROOM

Serves 8

1 cup fresh sliced mushrooms
2 Tablespoons butter
2 Tablespoons flour
1/4 cup grated Parmesan cheese
1 cup hot milk
2 cups ground cooked ham
1 pound ground veal (or beef or pork)
1 green pepper, diced
1 onion, grated
2 eggs
1/2 cup bread crumbs
1/2 teaspoon salt
1/4 teaspoon pepper

Saute mushrooms in butter. Blend in flour. Stir in hot milk. Cook until it thickens and is smooth. Stir in Parmesan cheese. Set aside. In a bowl combine ham, veal, green pepper, onion, eggs, bread crumbs, salt and pepper. Blend well. Spread half of the mixture in a buttered gratin dish. Pour half of the mushroom sauce on top. Add remaining meat mixture, then remaining sauce. Bake in pre-heated oven at 350°F for 45 minutes.

Freezes well.

135 CHICKEN LIVERS AU VIN

Serves 4

1 pound chicken livers (cut in half)
3 Tablespoons butter
1 onion, chopped
2 stalks celery, sliced
1 clove garlic, chopped
3 green onions, sliced
1/2 pound mushrooms, quartered
1 1/4 teaspoons salt
freshly cracked pepper
pinch of oregano
1 Tablespoon finely chopped fresh parsley
1 Tablespoon chives
2 pinches marjoram
1/4 teaspoon basil
2 tomatoes, seeded and chopped
1/4 cup beef stock
1/2 cup dry red wine

In a heavy frying pan melt the butter, add the chicken livers, and fry lightly on medium heat. They should be rosy pink inside. Remove. To the butter and pan juices add the onion, celery, and garlic. Brown lightly and add the green onions and mushrooms. Cook for 2 minutes. Place the livers in the pan with the remaining ingredients. Simmer for 10 minutes and serve over buttered noodles, or garnished with toast points.

136 SPAGHETTI SQUASH PRIMAVERA

*Serves
10-12*

1 small spaghetti squash

Place in pan with 1" water and bake whole, at 375ºF for 1 hour or until flesh tests tender when poked with a skewer. Remove from oven. Let stand fifteen minutes.

Meanwhile make sauce:
1 cup butter
2 medium onions, diced
1/2 pound mushrooms, sliced
1 small clove garlic, minced
1 1/2 cups broccoli flowerettes
1 cup small peas
1 medium zucchini, sliced
4 carrots cut on the diagonal

(continued)

1 1/2 cups whipping cream
1/2 cup chicken stock
1/4 cup fresh basil leaves
    (or 1 Tablespoon dried)
1 sweet red pepper, sliced
6 green onions, chopped
12 slices cooked bacon
1 1/2 cups freshly grated Parmesan cheese
12 cherry tomatoes

In a large frying pan put butter, onions, mushrooms and garlic. Saute gently until onion is soft.

Add broccoli, peas, zucchini and carrots.

Add cream, stock and basil. Salt and pepper to taste. Boil briskly to evaporate sauce a little. Add green onions, bacon, cherry tomatoes and cheese. Heat thoroughly and serve immediately.

To assemble: carefully cut hot squash in half lengthwise. Remove seeds and with a fork remove strands of squash. Place in hot shallow casserole. Top immediately with hot sauce. Pass extra Parmesan if desired.

FRITTATA VERDE (GREEN OMELET) 137

Serves 2-4

6 slices bacon
1 medium onion, thinly sliced
1 cup finely chopped raw spinach
6 eggs
1/4 cup grated Parmesan cheese
1 Tablespoon chopped parsley
1 clove garlic, finely minced
1 teaspoon salt
1/8 teaspoon freshly grated pepper

Preheat oven to 350°F. In an eight inch, heavy skillet, with oven proof handle, fry bacon until crisp. Remove bacon, crumble and set aside. In bacon fat, saute onions until soft and golden. In a bowl combine bacon, eggs, spinach, Parmesan cheese, parsley, garlic, salt and pepper and beat with wire whisk until frothy. Pour over onions in hot skillet and cook on top of stove for about three minutes, lifting around edges with spatula to let liquid run underneath. Place in preheated oven and bake, uncovered, for about ten minutes or until top is set. Loosen around edges and slice omelet onto serving platter. Cut in wedges.

CHEF BRUNO'S "SPECIAL OF THE DAY" (CHICKEN HUNTER STYLE)

Serves 8

2 fresh spring chickens
(about 2 pounds each)
1/2 ounce dried Italian mushrooms
1/2 cup warm water
2 Tablespoons tomato paste
1/4 cup vegetable oil
1/4 cup butter
1/2 pound onions, diced
2 cloves garlic, mashed
1 teaspoon fresh rosemary
1-1 1/2 bay leaves, crumbled
1/2 teaspoon ground black pepper
3/4 cup dry white wine
2 medium tomatoes, chopped fine
1 ounce good brandy

Cut chicken into serving pieces. Soak dried mushrooms in warm water for 15 minutes. Drain, saving the water, and chop the mushrooms. Stir the tomato paste into the mushroom water. In a large skillet or pot heat oil and butter. Add onions and cook gently until soft and golden. Add chicken pieces and brown for 10 minutes. Add garlic, rosemary, bay leaves and pepper. Stir and cook for 5 minutes.

Add wine, cover and simmer slowly for 5 more minutes. Add tomatoes, mushrooms and mushroom water with tomato paste. Cook for 15 minutes, uncovered. Never overcook chicken. Stir the brandy into the sauce. Taste for salt.

Serve on large platter with freshly cooked spaghettini and sauce spooned over all.

"FLORIA TOSCA" ROMAN CASSEROLE 139

Serves 6-8

1 pound Bocconcini (macaroni
    shaped pasta)
1 — 14 ounce can whole tomatoes
2 green onions, chopped
2 stalks celery, chopped
1 cup fresh sliced mushrooms
3 Tablespoons butter
1/4 teaspoon salt
1/8 teaspoon pepper
1/2 cup each of three kinds of
    cheese: grated Romano cheese,
    Ricotta (Italian cottage cheese)
    and mozzarella
3 eggs, beaten

Boil the macaroni in 4 quarts of salted water for 10 minutes (al dente). Drain and put in a large buttered baking dish. Melt butter and saute the onions, celery and mushrooms. Add tomatoes, salt and pepper. Simmer until well blended, about 10 minutes. Beat the eggs with the cheeses and add to the macaroni. Pour the sauce on top. Bake in a very hot oven — 450ºF for about 15 minutes. Put under broiler for a few minutes to brown.

A plate of antipasto, crusty Italian bread, Caesar salad — MAGNIFICO!

STUFFED PORK CHOPS 140

Serves 4

8 pork chops, 1/2 inch thick,
    bone in, fat on
1 cup dry bread crumbs
1/2 cup orange juice
1/4 cup milk
1/2 cup onions, chopped
1/2 teaspoon sage

Salt and pepper pork chops.

Heat orange juice, add milk and add to bread crumbs, onions and sage. Place mixture on pork chop, secure second pork chop on top with tooth picks and bake on rack in covered Dutch oven at 325ºF for 1 1/2 hours. Dutch oven should have water below the rack but not touching the chops.

Uncover casserole last 20 minutes in order to brown the pork chops.

141   PAGLIA E FIENO (STRAW AND HAY)

Serves 6

1/2 pound egg fettuccine (broad noodles)
1/4 pound spinach fettuccine
1 pound fresh mushrooms, sliced thin
1 cup fresh or frozen peas
salt
pepper
1 cup prosciutto (Italian ham)
4 Tablespoons butter
1 1/2 cups heavy cream, warm
1/2 cup chicken stock, warm
1 cup freshly grated Parmesan cheese

In a large skillet saute mushrooms and ham in butter. Add peas. Season with salt and pepper. Add 1/2 cup of the cream and simmer gently for about two minutes. Set aside. Cook the noodles separately in two large pots of salted boiling water. Do not overcook. This takes about seven minutes. Drain. In one pot mix both kinds of fettuccini and the cream sauce. Add 1/2 cup of Parmesan cheese and toss lightly. Add the chicken stock. Toss again. Add the rest of the cream and Parmesan cheese. Toss and serve immediately.

142   BAKED STEAK

1 — 3 inch thick sirloin steak
1/2 teaspoon salt
1/4 teaspoon ground pepper
1 garlic clove, minced
1 cup catsup
3 Tablespoons Worcestershire sauce
1/2 cup water
1 Tablespoon lemon juice
1 large Bermuda onion, sliced

Place steak in shallow roasting pan and brown under broiler on one side. Season with salt and pepper. Turn meat over, season with remaining ingredients. Bake 350ºF uncovered — about 1 hour for medium-well done. Check with meat thermometer. Cut in narrow strips.

LINGUINE WITH CLAM SAUCE   143

1 can whole clams
1 can minced clams
1 can shrimp (optional)
1 can Dungeness crab (optional)
1 medium onion, chopped fine
1 clove garlic, mashed
2 teaspoons olive oil
3 dashes Tabasco
1/2 cup dry white wine
2 cups chicken broth
freshly ground pepper
1 pound linguine noodles
6 ounces cream cheese
grated Parmesan cheese
fresh parsley
1 teaspoon oregano

Open cans, but do not drain juice from clams. In a 4 quart saucepan saute garlic in hot oil. Do not brown. Add onion and saute until soft. Add wine and chicken broth then seafood and juices from clams. Add seasoning, and let simmer 25 minutes. Meanwhile cook linguine in boiling water, salted, until al dente.

Cut cream cheese into small pieces, and when sauce is cooked add cheese, and blend into the sauce.

When linguine is cooked, drain well and add to the sauce. Allow pasta to rest in sauce for 2-3 minutes to absorb flavors.

Serve on a large, hot platter, sprinkle with Parmesan cheese and serve immediately.

144   CASSEROLE FROM THE SEA

Serves 6

2 cups shell noodles (cook
    according to instructions —
    drain well)
1 — 10 ounce can mushroom soup
1/3 cup mayonnaise or Miracle Whip
1/3 cup milk
1 — 4 ounce can shrimp (medium)
1 can tuna, 4 ounce size
1 can water chestnuts drained and sliced
1 cup chopped celery
3 Tablespoons chopped parsley — fresh
    (2 Tablespoons dry)
1/2 cup minced onion
1 teaspoon curry — or more according
    to taste
1 teaspoon Worcestershire sauce

Combine ingredients in buttered casserole.

Bake 30 minutes at 350°F.

145   SCALLOPS ST. GEORGES

Serves 4

1 onion, sliced
1 carrot, sliced
2 stalks of celery, sliced
6 peppercorns
1/2 teaspoon salt
1 cup water
1/2 cup dry white wine
juice of 1 lemon
1 pound scallops
2 Tablespoons butter
2 Tablespoons flour
1/3 cup cream
2 Tablespoons sherry

Make a stock using the onion, carrot, celery, peppercorns, salt, water, wine and lemon juice by placing them in a pan. Heat to boiling and then simmer for twenty minutes. Strain.

In the strained stock gently poach the scallops five minutes. Strain. Keep the scallops warm and reduce the stock to 1 cup by boiling rapidly.

In a separate pan melt the butter. Add the flour and mix well. Off the heat add the stock in small amounts. Heat to thicken the sauce over low heat. Add the cream gradually and the sherry and finally the scallops. Heat gently. Serve over rice.

BLENDER PECAN TORTE 146

Make this recipe twice:

2 Tablespoons all-purpose flour
2 1/2 teaspoons baking powder
4 eggs
3/4 cup white sugar
1 cup pecans or walnuts

Grease 4 — 2" x 8" round cake pans with shortening and line the bottoms with wax paper. Preheat oven to 350ºF.

Mix flour and baking powder. Put eggs and sugar in blender or food processor, cover and whirl. Add nuts and process until fine.

Add flour mixture and blend until just well mixed. Pour into the 2 pans and bake 350ºF for 35 minutes.

Repeat procedure for other 2 layers.

When cooked turn out and peel off the waxed paper immediately. Cool completely.

Mocha Cream Icing for the Torte —
Make at serving time
1/2 cup berry sugar
1/4 cup cocoa
1 Tablespoon instant coffee granules
1/2 teaspoon salt
2 teaspoons vanilla
2 1/2 cups cold whipping cream
1 package whip-it whipping cream stabilizer
1 Tablespoon (or to taste) of cognac,
      coffee liqueur or rum

Place ingredients in blender and whip until thick. This takes only a few seconds. Do not over blend. Ice between layers and over top and sides.

This Mocha Cream is great used alone in small sherbet glasses. It may also be frozen for superb mocha ice cream. A versatile recipe!

147 GINGERBREAD

1/4 cup butter
1/2 cup sugar
1 egg
1/4 cup table molasses
1/4 teaspoon cinnamon
1 cup flour
1/2 cup boiling water
1 teaspoon soda

Cream butter and sugar. Beat in egg and molasses. Combine cinnamon and flour. Dissolve soda in boiling water. Add dry ingredients alternately with soda-water combination. Combine well. This batter is very thin. Pour into greased and buttered 9" round layer cake pan.

Bake 400°F for 20-25 minutes.

Serve warm cut in wedges with Apples Pronto or September Sauce.

Note: There is no ginger in this cake.

148 APPLES PRONTO

Serves 8

5 large tart apples
3 Tablespoons melted butter
lemon juice
1/4 cup brown sugar
2 teaspoons brandy
cinnamon

Peel apples — core — cut into quarters.

Place apples, cut side down in buttered 8" x 8" pyrex or other heavy casserole. Drizzle melted butter over all, sprinkle with lemon juice, brown sugar, brandy and cinnamon. Bake uncovered, 400°F 20-25 minutes or until apples are tender. Remove from oven — stir gently to cover with sauce.

Serve warm with gingerbread or by itself with pecan ice cream over top.

149 SEPTEMBER SAUCE

2 cups whipping cream
3 Tablespoons dark brown sugar
1/2 teaspoon maple flavoring

(continued)

Stir ingredients together but do not whip. Chill until serving time then whip until stiff. Serve over warm gingerbread.

Top with toasted pecans.

Enough sauce to serve 12.

GRAPES IN BRANDY   150

Serves 4

3/4 cup liquid honey
6 Tablespoons brandy
1 Tablespoon lemon juice
1 pound green seedless grapes,
    stemmed
1 cup sour cream

Mix honey, brandy and lemon juice. Add grapes. Place in a plastic bag and seal tightly. Store in refrigerator. Serve in chilled sherbet glasses, topped with sour cream.

FUDGE PIE   151

Serves 8

1 cup sugar
1/2 cup butter
2 egg yolks
1 teaspoon vanilla
1/3 cup flour
2 or 4 squares unsweetened chocolate, melted
1/8 teaspoon salt
2 egg whites, beaten stiff

Cream sugar, butter, egg yolks and vanilla.

Add slightly cooled chocolate.

Blend in flour, fold in beaten egg whites with salt.

Spread in greased and floured, 8" pie plate.

Bake at 325°F for 35 minutes or until done.

Serve warm with ice cream.

152   ZUPPA INGLESE (ITALIAN TRIFLE)

sponge cake, baked in three 8" layer
    pans or purchased sponge cake layers
1/2 cup sweet dark rum
4 cups light cream
1 cup heavy cream, whipped
2 ounces semi-sweet chocolate, melted
6 Tablespoons cornstarch
6 egg yolks
6 Tablespoons sugar
1 teaspoon vanilla

Mix sugar and cornstarch and blend in the light cream. Bring to a boil in a double boiler, stirring constantly. Cook until mixture is very thick.

Blend a little custard into egg yolks, then mix yolks into the rest of the custard and continue to cook over simmering water until very thick, stirring to prevent curdling. Remove from heat and stir in vanilla. Pour 1/3 of custard into separate bowl and beat in melted chocolate. Cover. Let custards cool.

Meanwhile, cut each cake layer into halves horizontally and sprinkle with rum. Alternate vanilla and chocolate custards between cake layers beginning and ending with vanilla.

Cover and chill at least 24 hours. Just before serving cover cake with whipped cream and garnish with glace cherries, soaked in rum.

153   IRISH COFFEE ICE CREAM

Serves 6

1 pint coffee ice cream
3 Tablespoons instant espresso
    coffee granules
3 Tablespoons Irish Whiskey

Soften ice cream a little by stirring quickly. Dissolve coffee granules in whiskey. Stir into ice cream. Pack into plastic container, cover tightly and store in freezer.

Garnish with shaved chocolate and a candy coffee bean.

LEMONADE BIRTHDAY CAKE   154

Serves 12

1 — 10" angel cake
1 quart vanilla ice cream
1 — 6 ounce can frozen pink lemonade
1 cup whipping cream
chocolate curls

Slice cake into 3 even layers. Stir ice cream a little, quickly mix in frozen pink lemonade. Spread between layers. Freeze cake. When ready to serve cover with sweetened whipped cream, top with big chocolate curls. Add lighted* birthday candles and sing to the birthday person.

*Candles' heat may melt chocolate curls so leave some space between the two.

To make Big Chocolate Curls

Melt 1 small package semi-sweet chocolate chips over low heat.

Turn chocolate out onto back of jelly roll pan.

Cool in freezer for a very few minutes — just until chocolate sets but is not firm or cold. With a broad spatula, held at a 45° angle to the pan, gently scrape the chocolate off pan, pulling blade of spatula toward you in one steady motion. Chocolate should lift and curl as you move spatula. The curls should be stored in refrigerator until time to serve.

MARMALADE SOUFFLÉ   155

4 egg whites
2 Tablespoons white sugar
4 Tablespoons orange marmalade

Beat egg whites well, adding sugar gradually. Continue beating until stiff. Add marmalade and mix well.

Cook 1 hour or longer in top of well buttered double boiler with tight fitting lid (butter inside of lid too).

It can be cooked for well over the hour as long as water is simmering in bottom of double boiler. (Be sure it doesn't boil dry).

Do not remove lid even though it may rise above pot.

Serve with whipped cream flavored with sherry or rum.

This recipe can be doubled.

156   A LITTLE FROZEN FUN

Serves 4

2 bananas sliced very thinly
1/4 cup cold orange juice

Place banana slices on cookie sheet in freezer until frozen very hard.

Use spatula to remove slices.

Place in food processor with orange juice.

Blend until thick and creamy.

Serve immediately in small frosty-cold sherbet glasses.

Garnish with fresh strawberries.

157   GRANITA DI CAFFE (FLORENTINE)

Serves 4

4 Tablespoons instant coffee (use
    black roasted coffee or instant
    coffee for a possible deeper flavor)
2 cups boiling water
1/4-1/2 cup sugar or honey
2 teaspoons vanilla or 1 teaspoon
    aromatic orange bitters (angostura)
whipped cream (optional)

Combine instant coffee, boiling water, and 1/4 cup sugar (according to taste) in a saucepan.

Stir over medium heat until sugar is dissolved — do not boil. Cool . . . add vanilla or bitters.

Pour mixture into shallow pan and freeze until almost firm. Turn into chilled bowl and beat well . . . an electric beater will beat more air into mixture, thus making it lighter. Freeze until it is the consistency of sherbet.

Serve in chilled dessert dishes topped with a dollop of whipped cream sweetened with sugar and flavored with Tia Maria or Cointreau, depending on whether vanilla or orange bitters were used.

SHRIMP DIP 158

1 — 4 ounce package softened cream cheese
1 cup dairy sour cream
1 teaspoon onion salt
1 teaspoon prepared horseradish
1/2 teaspoon Worcestershire sauce
1 Tablespoon ketchup
1 teaspoon lemon juice
1 can broken shrimp — rinsed and drained

Mix cheese and sour cream thoroughly. Add other ingredients, adding shrimp last. Chill at least two hours.

CAVIAR DIP 159

1 — 3 ounce package cream cheese
1 cup sour cream
1/4 cup mayonnaise
2 teaspoons lemon juice
1/2 teaspoon dry mustard
3/4 teaspoon grated onion
1/4 teaspoon black pepper or lemon pepper
1/8 teaspoon salt
1/2 teaspoon dillweed
1 — 2 ounce jar salmon caviar (or whatever
    available — Danish Lumpfish Roe Caviar
    is good — red not black — shrimp also
    may be substituted)

Mix all ingredients well. Refrigerate to allow flavor to develop. Serve on crackers or toasted bread rounds or use as a dip for vegetables.

VEGETABLE DIP 160

1 cup mayonnaise
1 cup sour cream
1 Tablespoon chopped parsley
1 Tablespoon dill weed
1/4 cup chopped green onion
1 teaspoon Beau Monde seasoning

Blend all ingredients — let stand in refrigerator for a few hours. Serve with cut fresh vegetables — celery, cauliflower, carrots, zucchini, cherry tomatoes, Chinese pea pods.

161 PEPPERED PECANS

1/4 pound butter
1 pound shelled pecans (as large and uniform
    in size as possible)
1 Tablespoon salt
1/2 teaspoon white pepper

Preheat oven to 350ºF.

Melt butter in shallow baking pan.

Add pecans and stir well.

Bake 20 minutes stirring every 5 minutes.

Remove from oven and sprinkle with salt and pepper, stirring well to coat.

Let nuts cool in pan.

Remove to container.

162 WELCOME WAFERS

3/4 cup butter
1/2 cup shredded Cheddar cheese
1/3 cup blue cheese
1/2 clove garlic, minced
1 teaspoon parsley
1 teaspoon chives
2 cups sifted flour

Cream butter, Cheddar cheese and blue cheese. Set aside. Mix garlic, parsley, chives and flour. Combine two sets of ingredients.

Shape into one-half inch balls. Flatten with fork on cookie sheet.

Bake at 375ºF for 8 minutes or until slightly brown.

JALAPEÑO JELLY

4 (1/2 pint)

1 1/2 cups green bell peppers (chopped)
1 can (4 ounces) hot green chili peppers
1 1/2 cups vinegar
6 cups sugar
green coloring
1 bottle Certo

Put peppers and 1 cup vinegar in blender and mix until liquified. Pour mixture over 6 cups sugar in saucepan. Rinse jar with remaining 1/2 cup vinegar and add. Stir well and bring to a full rolling boil. Add 2 to 3 drops green coloring, then add 1 bottle Certo. Stir well. Remove from heat, skim if necessary. Pour into sterilized jars and seal.

To Serve:
Take 1 — 8 ounce block of Philadelphia cream cheese, pour pepper jelly over top and surround with crackers.

OYSTER BALLS

3 hard cooked eggs (2 if they are large)
1 can (2 1/2 ounce) smoked oysters
1/4 cup soft butter
1 teaspoon prepared mustard
1/4 teaspoon celery seed
1/2 teaspoon Worcestershire sauce
1/4 teaspoon parsley
1/2 teaspoon basil
Dash of lemon juice
bread crumbs

Chop eggs very fine.

Drain oysters very well.

Cream butter and blend in spices; add eggs and oysters; blend well.

Form into small balls and roll in very fine dry bread crumbs, preferably rye or brown. Place on plate and cover with plastic wrap and refrigerate.

Can be made a day ahead of time.

165   ROZ'S SHRIMP IN MARINADE

1 cup sour cream
1/4 cup cider vinegar
1/2 cup oil
1 teaspoon whole dill seed
1 teaspoon paprika
1/2 teaspoon ground pepper
2 Tablespoons prepared horseradish
2 Tablespoons grated onion
2 Tablespoons capers
Extra dill seed
Cold cooked and deveined whole shrimp

Blend all ingredients except shrimp and extra dill seed. Stir into shrimp, sprinkling extra dill seed over all (if desired). Chill for several hours to allow flavors to develop.

166   SCALLOPED OYSTERS

1/2 cup butter
1/2 cup flour
1 1/2 teaspoons paprika
1/4 teaspoon salt
Dash cayenne
1 large onion, chopped
1 1/2 cloves garlic, crushed
1/2 green pepper, chopped
1 teaspoon lemon juice
1 teaspoon Worcestershire sauce
1 quart chopped oysters
1/4 cup cracker crumbs

Cook and stir butter, flour, paprika, salt and cayenne for three minutes over medium heat.

Add onion, garlic and green pepper. Add to first mixture on stove. Cook another five minutes. Remove from stove.

Add lemon juice and Worcestershire sauce.

Heat chopped oysters gently in their juice.

Mix thoroughly with first mixture. Place in an 8" x 8" baking dish. Sprinkle with 1/4 cup cracker crumbs. Bake 30 minutes at 400°F.

Serve with soda bread, pumpernickel bread, or toasted bread rounds.

Freezes well.

KING CRAB CANAPES

2 — 6 ounce packages cream cheese
1 — 6 ounce package frozen king crab,
    defrosted and drained
1 Tablespoon mayonnaise
1/4 teaspoon salt or celery salt
1/4 teaspoon Worcestershire sauce
paprika
36 bread rounds, 1 1/2" diameter, toasted on
    one side

Beat the cream cheese until soft. Add crab meat, mayonnaise, salt and Worcestershire sauce. Mix thoroughly. Cover, refrigerate until ready to serve.

Cover bread rounds on untoasted side generously with crab meat mixture, sprinkle top with paprika. Place on cookie sheet under broiler. Broil until golden and bubbly. Serve very hot.

MUSHROOM PUFFS

Toasted bread rounds
1 — 6 ounce (250 gram) package Philadelphia
Cream Cheese
    (or onion cream cheese)
2 or 3 egg yolks
1 teaspoon Worcestershire sauce
About 36 medium sized mushrooms

Whip cream cheese, egg yolks and Worcestershire sauce until light and fluffy. Place a mushroom cap on toasted bread round or melba toast square, round side up. Cover completely with cheese mixture. Place on greased cookie sheet. Broil eight inches from broiler or bake at 425°F for 10-15 minutes or until brown and puffy.

May be frozen on cookie sheet, then stored in plastic bag until needed.

169   DEVILLED CHEESE BITES

1 — 3 ounce package cream cheese, softened
2 ounces blue cheese, crumbled
1 — 2 1/4 ounce can devilled ham
1/4 cup chopped pecans
1/2 cup snipped parsley
Pretzel sticks

Blend cheeses, devilled ham, pecans and chill.

Shape into small balls.

Roll in parsley.

Press pretzel stick handle into each ball.

Refrigerate until serving time.

170   COCKTAIL FRITTATA

Serves
18-24

6 green onions, finely chopped
5 Tablespoons butter
1/4 pound mushrooms, chopped
1/2 pound fresh spinach, minced
1 clove garlic, minced
1/4 teaspoon dried tarragon leaves
1/2 teaspoon fresh dill
3 Tablespoons dried parsley flakes
5 eggs
salt and pepper to taste
1/2 cup grated fresh Parmesan cheese

Heat oven to 425°F. Saute onions in 2 Tablespoons of the butter. Add mushrooms, saute 5 minutes.

Remove pan from heat, stir in spinach, garlic, tarragon and parsley. Cook over medium heat, stirring constantly until most of the liquid evaporates, about 5 minutes. Whisk eggs, combine with sauteed vegetables, salt, pepper and 1/4 cup cheese. Dot remaining butter in small tart pans (18-24 depending on size) heat in oven until butter sizzles. Spoon 2 Tablespoons of the egg mixture into each muffin pan, sprinkle with remaining cheese. Bake till puffed and light brown — 8-10 minutes. Let cool 1 minute — run knife around edge and remove. Serve immediately.

HOT CRAB DIP

2 — 8 ounce packages cream cheese
10 ounces Cheez Whiz
2/3 cup milk or dry sherry
1/2 teaspoon Worcestershire sauce
2 — 7 1/2 ounce cans crab meat

Soften cream cheese and add Cheez Whiz, milk (or sherry). Add Worcestershire sauce. Cook and stir until blended. Add crab meat. Serve warm, in a chafing dish, with wedges of Italian bread, or varieties of crackers and fresh vegetables.

LEMON CHICKEN WINGS

2 dozen chicken wings

Marinade

1/4 cup soya sauce
dash of gin or vodka
1 clove of garlic, crushed
1/8 teaspoon ginger

Clip wing tips and use to make chicken broth at another time. Separate remaining wing joints. Marinate overnight.

Sauce

1/4 cup sugar
1/2 cup lemon juice
1/4 teaspoon salt
1 Tablespoon cornstarch
1 Tablespoon oyster sauce (in Chinese Food
    section of your store)
1/4-1/2 cup water

Mix well. Place wing bones in large roaster. Baste with a little sauce. Cook at 400ºF for 20 minutes. Serve with remaining sauce.

173   CHEESE BREAD CUBES

Two loaves uncut sandwich bread, day old
1 carton Imperial sharp cheese
same amount of soft butter

Remove crusts from bread and cut bread into 2" cubes.

Bring cheese to room temperature and cream together with the butter.

Spread cheese mixture on three sides of bread squares — leave bottom without cheese mixture.

Sprinkle with paprika.

When ready to serve bake on greased cookie sheet at 350°F for approximately ten minutes.

Can be frozen, unbaked. Freeze by placing on cookie sheet. When solid, put squares into heavy plastic bag, tightly sealed.

174   ENGLISH MUFFIN WEDGES

Serves 12

1 1/2 cups shredded sharp Cheddar cheese
1 cup chopped green onions
1 cup chopped ripe olives
1 teaspoon curry powder
1/2 cup mayonnaise
1 package English muffins (about 8)

Mix first five ingredients together, spread on muffins. Cut each muffin in quarters. Pop under broiler for about 5 minutes or until bubbly and beginning to brown.

CRAB SUPREME

Microwave

2 — 3 ounce packages cream cheese
1 — 10 3/4 ounce can cream of mushroom
    soup
1 envelope unflavoured gelatine
3 Tablespoons cold water
1 green onion, finely chopped
1 cup finely chopped celery
1 cup mayonnaise
1 — 7 ounce can crab meat, drained and flaked

In a one quart measure, soften cream cheese for 45 seconds in a microwave oven.

Mix in soup and cook for three minutes.

Stir well and cook for another three minutes.

Dissolve gelatine in water.

Add to cheese mixture.

In mixing bowl combine onion, celery, mayonnaise and crab.

Blend thoroughly.

Pour into oiled mold.

Chill, and unmold.

POTTED CRAB

4 Tablespoons soft butter
2 Tablespoons mayonnaise
1 can crabmeat, drained
1/4 teaspoon mace
pinch of nutmeg
squeeze of lemon juice

Blend butter and mayonnaise. Flake crab and remove any shell. Beat into first mixture, adding remaining ingredients.

Pack tightly in a small crock.

Refrigerate, covered.

177   OVEN BAKED MEATBALLS

1 pound lean ground beef
1/8 teaspoon garlic salt
1/8 teaspoon pepper
3 Tablespoons minced onion
1/2 cup finely crushed chow mein noodles
1/2 cup milk
1/2 cup soya sauce
2 Tablespoons salad oil
1 clove garlic, crushed
1/2 teaspoon ground ginger
1 Tablespoon sugar

Combine ground beef, garlic, salt, pepper, onion, noodles and milk. Mix well. Shape mixture into balls, about 3/4" in diameter. Place balls in shallow baking dish.

Combine soya sauce, water, oil, garlic, ginger and sugar. Mix well.

Pour this mixture over meatballs. Marinate at least one hour, turning meat balls occasionally.

Bake balls, uncovered, in marinade in oven preheated to 350ºF about 30 minutes or until they are done. Insert wooden picks in balls and serve hot.

178   BLUE CHEESE PÂTÉ

1/4 pound blue cheese, softened
1/2 cup soft butter
1 clove garlic, crushed
1 Tablespoon minced parsley
2 green onions, finely chopped
3 — 4 Tablespoons brandy

Mix and pack into a jar. Refrigerate and when ready to use, serve with crisp crackers.

QUICHE LORRAINE TARTS   179

Yields: 36

4 eggs slightly beaten
1 1/3 cups sour cream
1 teaspoon salt
3/4 teaspoon Worcestershire sauce
1 1/3 cups grated Swiss cheese
2/3 cup chopped bacon
1/3 cup chopped onions

Line small tart shells with pastry.

Mix eggs, sour cream, salt, Worcestershire sauce and cheese together.

Saute bacon and onions together, drain off excess fat.

Divide evenly among tart shells.

Spoon egg-cream mixture on top.

Bake 15-17 minutes at 350ºF or until mixture is golden and set.

CHUTNEY CHEESE CROCK   180

Yields:
2 cups

2 — 8 ounce packages cream cheese
1/2 cup chutney
1/2 cup toasted chopped almonds
2 teaspoons curry powder
1/2 teaspoon dry mustard

Let cream cheese stand at room temperature to soften. Mix in chutney, chopped so there are no large pieces, and toasted chopped almonds.

Season with curry powder and dry mustard.

Mix until creamy.

Spoon into small crocks.

Refrigerate for several hours to bring out flavors.

May be varied with Macadamia nuts or pine nuts.

Serve with Melba toast, sliced apples.

SANDWICH FILLINGS
FOR A PROPER TEA

181 *SMOKED SALMON FINGERS*

1 cup chopped smoked salmon
2 Tablespoons finely chopped onion
½ teaspoon Dijon mustard
2 Tablespoons mayonnaise

Blend all ingredients. Spread on fresh cracked wheat bread, buttered. Cut in fingers and garnish with watercress and capers.

182 *CHICKEN OR TUNA ROUNDS*

Use to fill very fresh, moist whole wheat bread cut in rounds with a sharp cookie cutter.

1 cup finely minced, cooked chicken
   breast or 1 can white tuna,
   well drained
¼ cup finely chopped celery
1 teaspoon prepared mustard
3 Tablespoons mayonnaise
½ teaspoon minced onion
Salt, white pepper

Blend all ingredients. Spread on buttered bread, top with second round of bread. Keep moist in heavy plastic bags in refrigerator.

183 *WATERCRESS SANDWICHES*

Spread whipped creamed cheese on slices of fresh white bread. Sprinkle with chopped fresh watercress, add salt and pepper to taste. On second set of bread slices, spread a good mayonnaise (preferably homemade).

Top the watercress slices with the mayonnaise ones.

Pat firmly. Trim crusts, cut into triangles or squares.

BANNY MUFFINS

Yields: 12

1 1/2 cups unsifted flour
1 cup brown sugar, packed
1/2 teaspoon salt
2 teaspoons baking powder
2 eggs
milk
1 teaspoon vanilla

Blend dry ingredients. Put eggs in a measuring cup, add milk to 1 cup level. Add vanilla, beat. Add liquids to dry ingredients beating well. Pour mixture into medium sized greased muffin pans. Bake 375ºF 20 minutes or until top springs back when touched.

These are not showy — but when you've been gardening all day and need something sweet and sort of chewy — these can be ready by the time you shower and get the kettle going for tea.

BRAN MUFFINS

Serves 36

1 cup brown sugar, packed
1 1/4 cups corn oil
3/4 cup molasses
1/4 cup maple syrup
1/2 teaspoon salt
3 eggs
3 1/2 cups milk
4 teaspoons baking powder
4 teaspoons baking soda
4 cups whole wheat flour
4 cups bran
1 cup raisins and 1 cup pitted dates, chopped

Beat eggs, add sugar, molasses, maple syrup, salt, milk, corn oil, baking powder and soda. Mix well.

Add flour and bran. Blend. Add raisins and dates.

Grease and fill muffin tins 3/4 full.

Cook in 400ºF pre-heated oven 15-20 minutes.

Mixture seems to improve if left to stand in fridge for a day.

186 ANDREW'S MUFFINS

Yields: *48*

2/3 cup butter
1 cup white sugar
2 eggs, beaten
3 cups flour
1 Tablespoon baking powder
1 teaspoon salt
2 teaspoons nutmeg
1 cup milk

Cream first three ingredients. Combine dry ingredients. Add alternately with milk. Bake in very small muffin pans at 350ºF for 20 minutes. While hot, roll in melted butter then in mixture of white sugar and cinnamon. These muffins freeze well.

187 ORANGE AND DATE MUFFINS

1 whole orange
1/2 cup orange juice
1 egg
1/2 cup butter or margarine
1 1/2 cups all-purpose flour
1 teaspoon baking soda
1 teaspoon baking powder
3/4 cup sugar
1 scant teaspoon salt
1/2 cup chopped, pitted dates

Cut orange into pieces, remove seeds and drop pieces into blender. Blend till rind is finely ground. Add juice, egg and butter and give another whirl in blender. Into a bowl, sift flour, baking soda and baking powder, sugar and salt. Pour orange mixture over dry ingredients and stir lightly.

Add finely chopped dates. Spoon into 18 buttered muffin tins.

Bake at 400ºF for about 15 minutes.

TELEGRAPH HOUSE OAT CAKES

1/2 teaspoon baking soda
1/2 cup boiling water
1 1/4 cups sugar
2 cups quick-cooking rolled oats
2 cups flour
1 teaspoon baking powder
1 teaspoon salt
2 cups bran flakes
1 1/4 cups shortening

Add soda to boiling water and let stand until cool.

Mix together all of the dry ingredients. Cut in shortening. Add soda and water mixture and blend well.

Roll thin on floured board.

Cut in 4'' squares. Place on greased cookie sheet.

Bake 375ºF until golden brown and crisp.

COUNTRY LANE TEA BREAD

2 cups raisins
1 cup sugar
1 cup brown sugar, packed
1/4 cup cooking oil
1 Tablespoon molasses or corn syrup
4 teaspoons baking soda
2 1/2 cups boiling water
2 cups white flour
1 cup whole wheat flour
3/4 teaspoon salt
1 cup quick cooking oats

Mix raisins, sugar, oil, molasses, soda and water in large bowl. Leave overnight in a cool place. In the morning, add flour, salt and rolled oats. Beat together and put into two greased 9'' x 5'' bread pans. Let stand 15 minutes. Bake at 350ºF for 1 hour, or until done. Let cool in pans.

Try this, spread with orange cream cheese.

190   BLUEBERRY ORANGE COFFEE CAKE

1 — 11 ounce can mandarin orange sections
1 package blueberry muffin mix
1/4 cup brown sugar, packed
3 Tablespoons flour
2 Tablespoons firm butter or margarine
1/4 teaspoon cinnamon

Drain mandarin orange sections. Prepare blueberry muffin mix as directed. Pour batter into buttered quiche pan. Arrange orange sections over top.

Mix brown sugar, flour, butter and cinnamon to form a crumbly Streusel mixture.

Sprinkle on top of orange sections.

Bake at 400ºF for 25-30 minutes or until done.

191   PRINCIPAL'S CAKE

1 cup chopped dates
1 1/2 cups boiling water
1 teaspoon soda
1/2 cup shortening
1 cup sugar
2 eggs
1 1/2 cups flour
1/2 teaspoon salt
3/4 teaspoon soda
1 cup chocolate chips
3/4 cup brown sugar, packed
1/2 cup chopped walnuts

Pour boiling water over dates. Add soda. Let cool.

Cream shortening and sugar together. Add eggs and beat well. Add date mixture. Stir in flour, salt and soda which have been sifted together. Beat well and pour into greased 9" x 13" pan.

Sprinkle batter with chocolate chips, brown sugar and nuts.

Bake at 350ºF for about 45 minutes, or until done.

1/2 cup sugar
1/4 cup butter
1 egg
1 teaspoon vanilla
1 1/2 cups flour
1/4 teaspoon salt
2 teaspoons baking powder
2/3 cups milk
1 cup pecan halves
brown sugar
butter

Cream sugar and butter. Add egg and vanilla, whipping until light and fluffy. Blend dry ingredients and add alternately with milk.

Spread batter in greased 9" pan.

Spread pecan halves over top.

Sprinkle with a generous layer of brown sugar — almost covering the pecans.

Dot with butter.

Bake 375ºF for 25 minutes or until cake tester comes out clean.

Serve warm in large wedges.

Freezes well.

SOUR CREAM COFFEE CAKE

Step 1

2 squares unsweetened chocolate, grated
1 teaspoon cinnamon
1/2 cup white sugar
1/2 cup chopped nuts

Combine and set aside

Step 2

1 cup margarine or butter
1 1/2 cups white sugar
5 large eggs

Cream margarine and blend in sugar. Beat in eggs one at a time, beating until light after each.

Step 3

3 cups sifted all purpose flour
1 teaspoon baking soda
2 teaspoons baking powder
3/4 teaspoon salt
1 cup plus 2 Tablespoons commercial sour cream
1 teaspoon almond extract
1 teaspoon vanilla

Sift together flour, baking soda, baking powder and salt. Add to margarine mixture alternately with cream, beating after each addition. Add almond and vanilla extracts. Spoon one half of batter into well greased ten inch tube pan and sprinkle with one half of the chocolate mixture. Top with remaining batter and sprinkle with remaining chocolate mixture. Cut through batter to marble. Batter is stiff. Bake at 350ºF for one hour.

(Check at fifty minutes — may be done then).

POPPY SEED LOAF

Yields:
2 loaves

6 eggs
2 cups sugar
1 1/4 cups oil
1 cup poppy seeds
1/2 cup milk
2 cups flour
2 teaspoons baking powder
1/2 teaspoon salt
1 teaspoon vanilla
2 teaspoons almond extract
1 cup chopped walnuts

Beat eggs until thick and light, add sugar and oil, and poppy seeds and milk.

Blend flour and baking powder, salt — mix in. Add flavorings and nuts.

Pour into 2 greased and floured loaf pans.

Bake 325°F for 1 hour or until done.

PUMPKIN BREAD

1 1/2 cups flour
1 teaspoon baking powder
1 teaspoon baking soda
1/4 teaspoon salt
1 teaspoon cinnamon
1 cup sugar
3/4 cup corn oil
2 eggs, beaten
1 cup canned pumpkin
1/2 cup raisins

Sift together first five ingredients. Set aside. Mix sugar and oil, add eggs and pumpkin. Add dry ingredients and raisins. Blend well. Pour into greased and floured loaf pan (4" x 9") and bake 350°F for 50-60 minutes.

196   RAISIN COFFEE CAKE

Note: This coffee cake starts in a cold oven.

1 cup butter
1 1/4 cups white sugar
1 teaspoon vanilla ·
2 eggs
1 cup commercial sour cream
2 cups flour
1/2 teaspoon soda
1 1/2 teaspoons baking powder
3/4 cup raisins
1 teaspoon cinnamon
2 Tablespoons brown sugar

Cream butter and sugar well. Add vanilla.

Add eggs and beat until light. Blend in sour cream. Sift flour, soda and baking powder and add to creamed mixture.

Spoon half of batter into pan (angel cake pan or a large bread tin) which has been buttered and floured. Sprinkle half raisin, cinnamon, sugar mixture over batter. Spoon in remaining batter and top with rest of raisin mixture.

Put into *cold oven* and set at 350ºF.

Bake for one hour.

197   MOCHA LOAF

2/3 cup shortening
2 cups sifted cake flour
1 1/4 cups sugar
1 Tablespoon instant coffee
1 teaspoon salt
1/2 teaspoon cream of tartar
1/4 teaspoon soda
1/2 cup water
1 teaspoon vanilla
3 eggs
2 squares unsweetened chocolate,
    melted

Cream shortening. Blend in all dry ingredients together. Add water and vanilla and beat until well mixed — about 2 minutes

(continued)

with a mixer. Add eggs and chocolate. Beat 2 minutes longer. Prepare pan by greasing and lining with waxed paper. Pour batter into pan (9 1/2" x 5" x 3").

Bake 325°F for 65-70 minutes or until done. Cool 15 minutes then cool on cake rack. Frost with vanilla icing.

CARAMEL ROLLS   198

4 teaspoons baking powder
1/2 teaspoon salt
2 cups flour
1/2 cup shortening
3/4 cup milk
soft butter
1/3 cup brown sugar
1 Tablespoon cinnamon
1/4 cup butter
1/3 cup packed brown sugar

Sift first three ingredients. Add shortening. Mix until resembles coarse meal.

Add milk and beat long enough to form soft dough.

Place dough on floured board and knead lightly.

Roll out to 1/2 inch thickness. Spread with soft butter, sprinkle with brown sugar and cinnamon.

Roll like jelly roll and slice 1/2 inch thick.

Place in pan lined with the following: 1/4 cup melted butter and 1/3 cup firmly packed brown sugar.

Bake 15 minutes at 450°F. Remove from oven and immediately turn out onto a plate and serve hot. 1/4 cup currants can be added to filling.

199 NO-KNEAD HEALTH BREAD

2/3 cup warm water
2 teaspoons honey
2 envelopes active dry yeast
5 cups whole wheat flour
3 Tablespoons molasses
1 cup lukewarm water
1/2 teaspoon salt
1/3 cup wheat germ
1/3 cup bran
1 1/2 cups lukewarm water

Stir 2 teaspoons of honey in 2/3 cup water.

Sprinkle yeast on top and set aside until it bubbles.

Warm flour by placing in a 250ºF oven for about 15 minutes.

Combine molasses with 1 cup warm water and stir in the bubbly yeast mixture.

Stir in warmed flour, salt, wheat germ, bran and the 1 1/2 cups warm water. Mix well but don't knead, dough is sticky.

Grease a 9" x 5" loaf pan and turn dough into this. Grease top. Leave in a warm place till dough rises to the top of pan.

Bake in a 400ºF oven for about 40 minutes.

Set pan on a rack to cool, for about 10 minutes. Remove from pan and cool completely before slicing.

Excellent with baked beans or a cheese spread.

200 SODA BREAD

2 cups flour
1/2 cup bran
1 1/2 cups whole wheat flour
2 1/2 teaspoons soda
2 1/2 cups buttermilk or yogurt
Salt to taste
1/4 cup brown sugar, packed

Mix flour, bran, whole wheat flour and soda together. Add buttermilk or yogurt, salt and brown sugar. Bake in *small* well greased bread pan at 350ºF for 1 1/2 hours.

Good served with caviar dip or scalloped clams.

LACE WAFERS

1/4 cup brown sugar
1/4 cup corn syrup
1/4 cup margarine or butter
1/8 teaspoon salt
1/4 teaspoon baking powder
2 cups sifted all-purpose flour
1/2 cup flaked coconut
1/2 teaspoon vanilla

Combine sugar, syrup and butter in saucepan. Cook, stirring constantly until mixture boils. Boil one minute and remove. Combine dry ingredients and mix into syrup mixture. Add vanilla. Drop 1 tablespoon of batter on greased cookie sheet. Bake four at a time at 350ºF for 8 minutes. Cool 1/2 minute and roll around handle of wooden spoon. Fill with whipped cream just before serving.

CHOCOLATE DREAM BARS

1/2 cup butter
3 Tablespoons sugar
1/4 cup cocoa
1/4 teaspoon salt
3/4 cup flour
2 eggs, beaten
1 1/2 cups brown sugar, packed
3 Tablespoons flour
1/2 teaspoon salt
1 teaspoon baking powder
1 teaspoon vanilla
1/2 cup coconut
1 cup chopped walnuts

Base:
Mix butter, sugar, cocoa, salt and flour, and press into 9" x 9" greased pan. Bake 300ºF for 20 minutes or until firm.

Topping:
Blend the rest of the ingredients and pour over baked base. Bake at 275ºF for 30-35 minutes. Does not need frosting.

203   CHEESE AND CRAB APPLE JELLY SQUARES

1 cup cold butter or margarine
1 Tablespoon brown sugar
1/4 pound Imperial cheese chilled
1 1/2 cups flour
1 teaspoon baking powder
1/2 teaspoon salt
crab apple jelly (1 small jar)

Cream butter, sugar and cheese. Cut in dry ingredients, as for pastry (fine crumbs). Blend well.

Pat 3/4 of mixture into an 8" x 8" pan.

Spread with crab apple jelly to cover well.

Sprinkle balance of cheese mixture over top and pat down.

Bake 350ºF for 30 minutes. Top should be slightly brown. Chill before cutting.

204   KAFFLINGS

Yields: 84

1 1/2 cups butter
1 cup fruit sugar
1/2 teaspoon vanilla
1 1/2 cups almonds, ground
3 cups flour
icing sugar

Cream butter, sugar, vanilla and ground almonds. Add flour, working it in well with the hands until mixture is smooth and holds together when squeezed. Shape into crescents, about thumb size.

Place on cookie sheets covered with greased wax paper, and bake at 275ºF 40 minutes.

Roll in icing sugar while still warm.

One of the very nicest cookies that can be served. They melt in your mouth.

THOSE CHOCOLATE MACAROONS

3 squares unsweetened chocolate
1 can sweetened condensed milk
1 package long-shred sweetened coconut
1 teaspoon vanilla

Melt chocolate, add milk and stir until mixture looks like pudding. Take off heat, add coconut and vanilla, mixing well.

Spoon in mounds on well greased cookie sheet.

Bake 325°F for 6-8 minutes or until macaroons appear to be set.

Let stand a minute then carefully remove macaroons to cake racks. Cool completely. Store in airtight container.

ROMANCE CAKE

Base:
1 cup flour
1/2 cup butter
2 Tablespoons white sugar

Topping:
1 1/4 cups brown sugar, packed
2 eggs, beaten
1/2 cup coconut
2 Tablespoons flour
1/2 teaspoon baking powder
1 teaspoon vanilla
1 cup raisins
1/2 cup glazed cherries (cut)
1/2 cup nuts, walnuts or pecans

Base:
Mix and press into an 8" x 8" square pan.

Bake 15 minutes at 350°F.

Topping:
Mix topping together.

Pour over partially cooked base.

Bake 20 minutes (top should be set) at 350°F.

When cool sprinkle with icing sugar or spread with lemon butter icing.

207 COFFEE RING

 2 cups flour
 1 Tablespoon baking powder
 3 Tablespoons sugar
 1/4 teaspoon salt
 1 cup shortening.

Blend ingredients, cutting in shortening as for pastry then add:

 1 egg
 1 teaspoon vanilla
 1/2 cup milk

Roll out a little thicker than pie crust. Divide into 2 rectangles. Sprinkle each rectangle with half of:

 1 cup brown sugar
 1 cup raisins and currants
 1/2 cup walnuts
 1 1/2 teaspoons cinnamon
 2 Tablespoons butter — dotted all over

Roll rectangles starting with long side. Secure edges well. Put into 2 pie plates, curving to fit plate. Plates should be greased. Bake 350°F for 30 minutes.

Dribble with coffee flavored icing while hot.

Freezes well.

208 OL' MACDONNELL'S MUNCHIES

 1/2 cup melted butter
 1 cup brown sugar
 2 cups rolled oats
 1/2 teaspoon salt
 1 teaspoon vanilla

Mix together. Press into 8 by 8 inch pan.

Bake 350°F for 20 minutes.

Cut in fingers while still warm.

DANISH PUFF

1 cup flour
1/2 cup butter
2 Tablespoons water
1/2 cup butter
1 cup water
1 1/4 teaspoons almond extract
1 cup flour
3 eggs
2 Tablespoons butter
1 cup icing sugar
lemon juice
grated lemon rind, toasted, chopped almonds

Mix flour, 1/2 cup butter and water. Roll into ball, divide in 2 and pat into two long strips 3" x 12" on a baking sheet. Need not be too perfect.

Bring second amount of butter and water to a full rolling boil. Add flavoring, then remove from heat and stir in the flour. Beat in 3 eggs, one at a time, beating vigorously until smooth and shiny. Place half of this mixture on each bottom crust strip. Bake at 350°F until puffed and golden brown, about 45 minutes.

Frost while warm with icing sugar mixed with the butter and thinned with lemon juice. Garnish with grated rind and chopped almonds. May be frozen.

FAST PECAN BARS

Yields: 24

2 Tablespoons butter
2 eggs, beaten
1 cup brown sugar, packed
5 Tablespoons flour
1/8 teaspoon soda
1 cup chopped pecans
1 teaspoon vanilla
icing sugar

Melt butter in 8" x 8" pan in heating oven — 350°F. Add beaten eggs to other ingredients except icing sugar. Pour carefully over butter. Do not stir. Bake about 20 minutes or until cake tests done. Turn out of pan onto rack. Dust with icing sugar.

211 ORANGE POPPY SEED CAKE

1 cup unsalted butter
1 1/2 cups sugar
4 large eggs
1 cup sour cream
2/3 cups poppy seeds
1/2 cup orange juice
2 Tablespoons grated orange rind
2 teaspoons vanilla
2 1/2 cups all purpose flour
1 teaspoon double acting baking powder
1/2 teaspoon baking soda
pinch of salt

In a bowl with an electric mixer, cream the butter and sugar until light and fluffy. Beat in eggs, one at a time, beating well after each addition. Add the sour cream, poppy seeds, orange juice and rind and the vanilla. Stir in the sifted dry ingredients and combine well.

Pour into a large buttered and floured tube pan or two loaf pans, and bake in a pre-heated 350ºF oven for 40 minutes or until done. Let stand for 5 minutes, then invert onto a rack, remove from pan and let cool completely. Dust with sifted confectioner's sugar and sprinkle with poppy seeds.

Tip:
A light dusting of fine bread crumbs, instead of flour, facilitates the removal of a cake from a Bundt pan.

212 FRENCH CHOCOLATES

Yields: 36

1 — 12 ounce package semi-sweet
   chocolate chips
1 cup walnuts, chopped
3/4 cups sweetened condensed milk
1 teaspoon vanilla
1/8 teaspoon salt

In a double boiler, over hot water, melt chocolate chips. Add remaining ingredients, stirring until slightly thickened. Cool until easy to handle.

With buttered hands shape into one inch balls.

Roll immediately in one cup chocolate sprinkles.

DRUNKEN DATE CAKE

1 pound chopped dates
1 cup chopped walnuts
1 teaspoon baking soda
1 cup boiling water
1/2 cup butter or margarine
1 cup brown sugar
2 eggs
1 cup flour
1/2 teaspoon salt
1 teaspoon vanilla
3 or 4 Tablespoons dark rum

Combine finely chopped dates, nuts, soda, and water and let stand until cool. Beat butter, sugar, and eggs; add to the first mixture; then add the flour, salt, and vanilla.

Bake in a greased tube pan at 350°F for 1 hour.

Drizzle with rum while cake is still warm.

Keeps well.

PARTY POUND CAKE

3 cups sifted flour
2 1/2 teaspoons baking powder
1/4 teaspoon salt
1 cup butter
1 1/2 cups sugar
2 eggs
2 egg yolks
1 cup milk
1 teaspoon vanilla
1/2 cup raisins

Sift dry ingredients together. Cream butter and sugar. Beat in eggs and egg yolks one at a time. Add vanilla. Add flour mixture alternately with milk and raisins ending with dry ingredients. Pour into greased and floured 9" tube pan or 2 loaf pans. Bake 350°F for 60-65 minutes or until cake tests done.

215 CHOCOLATE POUND CAKE

3 cups sifted flour
3 cups sugar
1 cup cocoa
1 Tablespoon baking powder
1 teaspoon salt
1 cup soft butter
1 1/2 cups milk
1 Tablespoon vanilla
3 large eggs
1/4 cup half and half

Sift dry ingredients into large bowl of mixer. Make a well in the center and add softened butter, milk and vanilla. Beat at low speed until blended, then beat at medium speed for 5 minutes, scraping down sides. At low speed add eggs one at a time, beating after each addition. Add cream and blend.

Pour batter into greased and floured 10" tube pan.

Bake 325ºF for 1 hour and 40 minutes or until done. Cool completely before removing from pan. **Do Not Invert Pan.**

216 MOCHA PEANUT CLUSTERS

Yields: 36

1/3 cup butter or margarine
1 — 6 ounce package semi-sweet chocolate
  pieces
1 — 4 ounce package full sized
  marshmallows (16)
1 teaspoon instant coffee powder or granules
2 cups chopped salted peanuts

Place butter, chocolate pieces and marshmallows in the top of a double boiler over simmering water. Cook, stirring occasionally until melted. Stir in peanuts. Line two cookie sheets with waxed paper. Drop rounded teaspoonfuls of the peanut mixture onto the wax paper. Cool and chill in refrigerator until hard.

PUMPKIN DATE TORTE 217

Serves 8

1/2 cup chopped dates
1/2 cup chopped walnuts
2 Tablespoons flour

1/4 cup butter
1 cup brown sugar
2/3 cup cooked pumpkin
1 teaspoon vanilla
2 eggs

1/2 cup sifted flour
1/2 teaspoon baking powder
1/2 teaspoon cinnamon
1/2 teaspoon nutmeg
1/4 teaspoon ginger
1/4 teaspoon baking soda

Mix dates, nuts and 2 tablespoons flour. Set aside.

Melt butter over low heat; blend in brown sugar. Remove from heat. Stir in pumpkin and vanilla. Beat in eggs, one at a time. Sift together the dry ingredients and add to pumpkin mixture, mixing thoroughly. Stir in floured dates and nuts. Turn into a greased 9 x 1 1/2 inch round baking pan. Bake 350°F for 20 to 25 minutes. Serve warm with whipped cream.

TINY PECAN TARTS 218

Yields: 48

8 ounces cream cheese
1 cup butter
2 1/4 cups flour
2 eggs slightly beaten
1 1/2 cups light brown sugar
2 teaspoons vanilla
1/2 teaspoon salt
2 cups chopped pecans

Blend together soft butter and cream cheese. Stir in flour and make into pastry dough. Divide into 48 balls. Press each ball into tiny muffin pans lined with paper cups. Combine eggs, sugar, vanilla and salt. Fold in nuts. Fill pastry shells and bake 25 to 30 minutes, or until filling is set, in 325°F oven.

219 MANDELTORTE

Pastry base:
1 1/4 cups flour
1 teaspoon baking powder
5 Tablespoons berry sugar
1/2 cup soft butter
1 egg, slightly beaten

Filling:
1/2 cup soft butter
1/2 cup berry sugar
1 cup finely ground almonds
1/2 teaspoon almond extract
2 eggs
1/3 cup raspberry jam

Pastry base:

Sift together dry ingredients. Cream butter with sugar, add egg. Blend in dry ingredients. Press into greased 10" spring form pan. Cover bottom and a little up the sides. Chill while mixing filling.

Filling:

In mixer, beat all ingredients together until light and fluffy. Spoon into prepared shell. Bake 350°F about 35-40 minutes — until golden and set.

Cool for one hour then spread with a generous 1/3 cup of the best raspberry jam. Drizzle lines of thin lemon icing to make squares over top. Cut in tiny wedges, as it is very rich. Green grapes go beautifully with this.

220 TEA ESSENCE

1 pound loose tea
10 cups boiling water

Let steep ten minutes. Strain and store covered tightly in refrigerator. When using essence use 1/2 cup essence to 8 cups boiling water.

Excellent for a large group.

TUNA MOUSSE

Serves 8

1 1/2 Tablespoons unflavored gelatine
1/2 cup cold water
1/4 cup lemon juice
1 cup mayonnaise
2 — 6 1/2 or 7 ounce cans white tuna, drained and coarsely flaked
1/2 cup cucumber, pared and chopped
1/2 cup thinly sliced celery
1/4 cup stuffed green olives, sliced
2 teaspoons onion juice
1 1/2 teaspoons prepared horseradish
1/4 teaspoon salt
1/4 teaspoon paprika
1 cup whipping cream

Soften gelatine in 1/2 cup cold water in saucepan.

Add lemon juice.

Heat and stir over medium heat till gelatine is dissolved.

In a bowl, combine mayonnaise and gelatine. Add tuna and remaining ingredients, except cream. Mix well. Fold in whipped cream.

Pour into an 8 1/2" x 4 1/2" x 2 1/2" oiled loaf pan.

Chill till firm.

Unmold. Serve with lime wedges.

FISH PÂTÉ

1 cup smoked salmon or smoked mackerel
1/4 cup soft butter
1/4 cup heavy cream
2 Tablespoons lemon juice
freshly ground black pepper

Mash the fish together with the butter and cream.

Add the lemon juice and lots of pepper.

Mix well together and refrigerate, covered, for several hours.

Serve on Melba toast.

223   DUCK PÂTÉ

2 ducks
8 Tablespoons brandy
8 Tablespoons Noilly Pratt Vermouth
8 Tablespoons Madeira
8 Tablespoons orange juice
2 bay leaves, crumbled
2 Tablespoons parsley
2 teaspoons grated orange rind
1 teaspoon thyme
1 onion, finely chopped
1 pound ground pork
1 pound ground veal
3 eggs
1 pound sliced bacon
oranges, thinly sliced

Roast ducks at 350ºF for 2 hours. When cool strip meat off bones and marinate in first 9 ingredients over night. Process the marinated mixture and the pork, veal, and eggs in the food processor. Season with salt and pepper to taste. Line pate dish with strips of bacon. Pour in ground meat mixture and cover with bacon.

Place terrine in a pan of hot water and bake in moderate oven (375ºF), about 1 to 1 1/4 hours.

Remove from oven and weight down pate so it compresses as it cools. Place foil on pate, then something heavy like a brick or heavy can of juice.

Packing Instructions
Wrap pate in foil and slice at picnic.

Serve with slices of orange, sprigs of watercress.

224   MELBA TOAST

Thinly sliced white bread (sourdough or French
   is good)
Butter

Spread bread slices with a generous amount of butter, including edges.

Place on racks on jelly roll sheets.

Bake 300ºF until crisp and golden.

Serves
10-12

1 pound ground lean pork
1/2 pound ground fat salt pork
1 pound pork liver
2 cloves garlic, chopped finely
6 green onions, chopped finely
1 teaspoon salt
1 teaspoon pepper
pinch of nutmeg
1/2 teaspoon thyme
3 eggs, beaten
bacon strips or salt pork
1 cup dry white wine
1 Tablespoon cognac

Combine ground pork, salt pork, pork liver, garlic, green onions, salt, pepper, nutmeg, thyme and beaten eggs and blend together thoroughly. Line a round or oblong casserole with strips of bacon or salt pork. Add the meat mixture, well packed down, and pour white wine and cognac over it. Press down again and top with additional strips of bacon or salt pork. Set the casserole in another pan as it may boil over. Cover and bake for 2 hours at 325ºF until thoroughly cooked. Remove from oven, uncover and weight the pate down so that it will have a more compact texture. Cool, remove weight and chill before serving. Remove fat and wrap in foil the day of the picnic.

CHICKEN TONNATO 226

Serves 6

3 whole chicken breasts,
   poached, sliced and chilled

Sauce:
1 1/2 cups mayonnaise
1 small can white tuna, drained
6 anchovy fillets, drained
2 Tablespoons lemon juice
3 Tablespoons capers

In food processor or blender place above ingredients, reserving 2 Tablespoons of the capers. Blend until smooth. Stir in remaining capers.

Arrange chicken slices on platter, spoon sauce over. Garnish with greens.

NOTE: This must be kept cold — so save this recipe for supper on a shady porch.

227 EGGS MIMOSA

12 eggs
2 — 7 ounce cans of crab meat
1/2-1 cup homemade mayonnaise
salt
freshly ground pepper
paprika
parsley

Simmer eggs until hard cooked and set in cold running water.

Drain crab and add mayonnaise till nicely moistened, but not wet.

Season with salt and pepper.

Peel eggs and cut in half lengthwise. Scoop out egg yolk and place in bowl.

Spoon into egg white, 1 teaspoon of crab mixture.

Sieve egg yolks over filled egg white and garnish with paprika and parsley. Chill.

228 GERMAN POTATO SALAD WITH SOUR CREAM

Serves 4-6   If you're on a diet, turn page quickly.

1 pound new potatoes, boiled in their jackets
1 teaspoon sugar
1/2 teaspoon salt
1/4 teaspoon dry mustard
freshly ground black pepper
2 Tablespoons vinegar
1 cup sour cream
1/2 cup thinly sliced cucumber
paprika

Slice potatoes in their jackets, while still warm.

Mix sugar, salt, mustard, pepper and vinegar.

Add sour cream and cucumber and blend well.

Pour sour cream mixture over the potatoes and toss lightly until all potatoes have been coated with the dressing.

Turn into a serving dish and sprinkle with paprika. Cool.

Serves 8

6 large zucchini, with skins
1 large sweet red pepper, chopped
1 large green pepper, slivered
6 green onions, including 6" of tops, chopped
1 cup mayonnaise
1 cup sour cream
salt, freshly grated black pepper

Shred zucchini in food processor. Drain thoroughly, patting dry between towels. Mix zucchini with remaining ingredients.

Line a round bowl (approximately 2 quarts) with plastic wrap. Pack salad into bowl, pressing down well.

Chill 2 or 3 hours, (no longer). To serve, place large flat platter over bowl containing salad. Quickly flip plate and bowl over, easing salad out of bowl. It should come out in a solid mound. Remove plastic wrap. Garnish plate with fresh vegetables and nasturtiums or other flowers.

COLD BEEF VINAIGRETTE   **230**

Marinate slices of cold rare roast beef in a vinaigrette dressing.

Serve on lettuce-lined platter with sliced peeled tomatoes, sweet onions, pickled beets and hard cooked eggs. Sprinkle vegetables with minced parsley and chives. Garnish with watercress.

Vinaigrette Dressing
2 teaspoons Dijon mustard
1 Tablespoon lemon juice
2 teaspoons sugar
1/2 cup vegetable oil
1 clove garlic, crushed
1 1/2 teaspoons sweet basil, minced
salt and fresh ground pepper to taste

In a small deep bowl, blend the mustard with the lemon juice and sugar. Whisk or beat in the oil, a few drops at a time, until the sauce is smooth and well blended. Stir in garlic and seasonings.

231 ORANGE, ONION SALAD, THE MOVEABLE FEAST

1 orange, skinned, cut into slices
1 red onion marinated in wine vinegar
1 butter lettuce or romaine

Yogurt Dressing
1 cup yogurt
1/4 cup sour cream
2 Tablespoons raisins
2 Tablespoons walnuts
4 slices of apple

Mix together first four ingredients. Arrange lettuce leaves on plate, then orange and onion overlapping each other.

Spoon dressing over salad.

232 CUCUMBER, CRAB SALAD

Serves 6

2 cucumbers, peeled
2 Tablespoons salt
2 cans crab or fresh crab to serve 6
2 Tablespoons Mirin*
1 Tablespoon sugar
2 Tablespoons rice vinegar
1/2 teaspoon M.S.G. (optional)

Cut cucumber in half lengthwise and scrape out seeds. Slice very thin. Sprinkle 2 Tablespoons salt over and set aside for 2 hours. Drain, rinse quickly. Squeeze out extra water. Pat dry.

Add crab meat, (reserving nice pieces for garnish).

Combine Mirin, sugar, rice vinegar and M.S.G. Stir until sugar dissolves. Pour over crabmeat and cucumber. Mix gently.

Allow to chill in refrigerator for at least 1 hour before serving.

*Mirin is found in the Oriental food section of your grocery store.

SPINACH SALAD

1 pound fresh spinach, trimmed, washed
1/2 pound mushrooms, sliced
1 can water chestnuts, drained and sliced
1 cup fresh bean sprouts
1/2 red onion, thinly sliced
1/2 cup Emmenthal cheese, shredded

Dressing
4 slices of bacon, cooked and crumbled
1/3 cup olive oil
2 Tablespoons Dijon mustard
1 Tablespoon white wine vinegar
1 garlic clove, minced
1 teaspoon sugar
salt and freshly ground pepper

Combine salad ingredients and chill in plastic bag till ready to pack.

Whisk together oil, mustard, vinegar, garlic, sugar, salt and pepper till emulsified. At serving time, toss dressing with salad.

TOMATO SALAD

Put slices of tomatoes on a platter with slices of red onion between each. Decorate plate with black olives and round slices of dill pickle. Sprinkle with fresh herbs of your choice — rosemary, sweet basil, oregano. Add crumbled Feta cheese if desired. Drizzle olive oil over all. Cover tightly and refrigerate for several hours before serving. Add fresh greens at serving time.

ARTICHOKES TITANIA

Serves 6

18 Artichoke hearts frozen, cooked or canned, drained
1/4 cup olive oil
2 Tablespoons white wine vinegar
2 Tablespoons lemon juice
1/4 teaspoon dried tarragon, crushed
1 teaspoon sugar
2 Tablespoons water
1/2 teaspoon dried oregano, crushed
1 garlic clove, crushed

Combine all ingredients in a bowl, cover and marinate overnight in the refrigerator.

Remove and drain in colander while making sauce.

Sauce:
2 cups sour cream
1/2 cup mayonnaise
1 teaspoon onion salt
2 ounces Philadelphia cream cheese
pinch tarrragon
1/8 teaspoon basil
pinch marjoram (optional)
pinch cayenne (optional, for the adventurous)
1/4 cup flaked cooked crab or cooked and deveined shrimp

Blend all ingredients except crab in food processor. Fold in crab or shrimp.

Keep cool.

At serving time pour sauce over drained marinated artichoke hearts.

1 head romaine, torn into small pieces
1 basket of white mushrooms, sliced
1 basket of bean sprouts or alfalfa sprouts
1/2 head celery, chopped (include some leaves)
3 green onions, sliced
2 sweet red peppers, cut in rings
1 bunch tiny radishes

Combine ingredients. At serving time, add dressing and place in a large ironstone bowl or wicker basket lined with plastic wrap.

Crown with a nosegay of fresh herbes and girdle with hard cooked eggs, sliced.

Accompany with rolls of smoked salmon filled with cream cheese, which has been spiked with horseradish and watercress; and ham slices rolled around German Potato Salad with Sour Cream.

Dressing
1/4 cup red wine
1/8 cup cider vinegar
1/4 cup salad oil
1 clove garlic, minced
1 teaspoon sugar
1 teaspoon salt
1/2 can chopped anchovies
1/2 cup bits cooked bacon
1/4 cup freshly grated Parmesan cheese

Blend first six ingredients. Toss salad. Add remaining ingredients.

VEGETABLE PÂTÉ

This recipe is extremely easy but the secret of success for the final presentation is to cool it thoroughly in the pan. When completely cool, it slides easily out of the pan intact. If still warm, the layers may not set and could break.

The Spinach Layer

4 — 9 ounce packages fresh spinach
4 eggs, beaten
dash salt and pepper
1/2 teaspoon nutmeg

The Tomato Layer

2 pounds ripe tomatoes
1/2 onion, chopped fine
1 teaspoon butter
2 cloves garlic, chopped fine
4 eggs, beaten

The Leek Layer

the whites of 5 leeks
1/2 pint of whipping cream
4 eggs, beaten
dash of salt

Boil water and blanche spinach for 2 minutes. Drain and rinse. Squeeze dry. Chop fine and mix with eggs and spices. Set aside. Blanche tomatoes, peel and seed. Chop coarsely. Saute onions, garlic, and tomato in butter until all moisture is gone. This requires about 45 minutes. Stir from time to time. Let cook, add eggs and spices, set aside.

Wash and chop leeks very fine. Blanche for 3 minutes. Strain and dry. Boil with cream until dry. When cool add eggs and spices.

Butter a 2 quart pate form well. Line bottom with buttered foil. Spread half of spinach mixture in bottom, followed by the tomato mixture on top, then a layer of the leek mixture and finally, the second half of the spinach mixture on top.

You will have four layers. Cover the form with greased foil. Set form in a pan with 1" water in bottom. Bake at 425°F for 1 3/4 to 2 hours or until set. Take out of oven and cool completely. Serve with horseradish-flavoured yogurt. This pate makes 15-20 slices.

Horseradish-Flavoured Yogurt

1 pint plain yogurt
1 Tablespoon horseradish
Combine ingredients well and serve.

RATATOUILLE

1 large firm eggplant
4 firm zucchini
1/2 pound (about 1 1/2 cups) chopped onions
4 cloves garlic, minced
1 pound fresh mushrooms, or 1 — 10 ounce
    can tiny button mushrooms
6 large tomatoes, skinned
1 small can tomato puree (5 1/2 ounce)
1 small can red peppers (pimentos)
1 generous teaspoonful herbes de provence
salt and pepper
olive oil

Peel eggplant and cut into cubes 1/2 inch square. Scrub zucchini well, slice off 2 ends and half or quarter pieces about the same size as the eggplant.

Place vegetables in bowl and toss with salt. Let stand 20-30 minutes. Drain and pat dry with towels.

Cover bottom of large skillet or electric frying pan with olive oil. Add onion and garlic and cook until transparent. Add eggplant and zucchini and gently saute until transparent, (add more oil if absorbing quickly). Transfer to fireproof casserole.

In same skillet, place tomatoes cut in 1/2 inch wedges. Cook until tomatoes begin to render their juices. Add salted mushrooms and lightly cook until mushrooms render juices.

When tomatoes are slightly mushy and mushrooms cooked, add a can of chopped red pimentos.

Sprinkle with herbes de provence and add more salt to taste and freshly ground black pepper.

Transfer to casserole and stir once or twice. Gently mix vegetables. Dilute tomato puree with equal amount of water and pour over vegetables.

Cover casserole and simmer over low heat for 15 minutes. Uncover and tip casserole and baste with combined tomato and rendered juices. Cook for 10 minutes more. Reheat slowly at serving time or serve cold.

239   MARINATED MUSHROOMS

1 pound fresh mushrooms
4 Tablespoons olive oil
1 Tablespoon lemon juice
1 garlic clove, minced
1 large onion, sliced
1/4 teaspoon thyme
1/4 teaspoon marjoram
1/4 teaspoon oregano
1 bay leaf
1 cup tomatoes, peeled, seeded, chopped
    and drained
1/3 cup wine vinegar
dash sugar
salt
pepper
few drops of Tabasco

Saute the mushrooms in 2 Tablespoons olive oil.

When golden, transfer to a bowl and toss with lemon juice.

Saute onions and garlic in remaining olive oil.

Add seasonings, tomatoes, vinegar, sugar, salt, pepper and Tabasco.

Bring to boil and simmer about 15 minutes.

Add marinade to mushrooms, cover tightly and refrigerate overnight.

240   TOURTIERE

Pastry for a 2 crust pie
1 pound raw minced pork
1 small onion, diced
1 small clove of garlic
1/2 teaspoon salt
1/2.teaspoon savoury
1/4 teaspoon celery salt
1/8 teaspoon pepper
1/4 teaspoon cloves
1/2 cup water

Combine ingredients in a heavy pot and bring to boil. Cook uncovered for 20 minutes or long enough to remove the pink

(continued)

color from the meat and to reduce most of the water, stirring frequently.

The mixture should appear damp and not watery.

Cool mixture and place in uncooked pie shell. Cover and seal with pastry.

Prick pastry to allow steam to escape and bake at 500°F for 15 minutes. Reduce heat to 350°F and bake until crust is light brown.

The tourtiere may be eaten now or you may wrap it in foil and freeze. When you want to serve it, bake the frozen pie at 350°F for 45 minutes.

Serve hot or cold with chili sauce or other relishes.

TABBOULEH (CRACKED WHEAT AND PARSLEY SALAD) 241

Serves 6-8

1 cup fine grain bulghur (cracked wheat)
1 cup minced parsley
2 tomatoes, chopped
1/2 cup fresh mint or 3 Tablespoons dried mint
1/3 cup scallions, thinly sliced
1/2 cup olive oil
1/4 cup lemon juice
salt and pepper
romaine leaves, chilled

Soak bulghur in boiling water for 1 to 2 hours or leave over night.

Drain bulghur and extract as much moisture as possible.

Place bulghur in large bowl and add parsley, tomatoes, mint and scallions.

In small bowl, mix oil with lemon juice, salt and pepper to taste and pour over mixture.

Traditionally a romaine leaf is used to scoop up a portion of bulghur, so you can line a serving bowl with romaine leaves and fill with tabbouleh when ready to serve.

SAVOURY FRENCH LOAF

1 loaf narrow French bread
4 large firm tomatoes
1 large onion
2 cloves of garlic
2 ounces black olives
3 ounces green olives
2 ounces gherkins or 2 ounces (8-10)
     drained anchovies
2 ounces capers
2 sweet green peppers
2 hard boiled eggs
sea salt
olive oil

Peel and seed tomatoes, drain upside down on rack.

Stone olives, seed peppers, press garlic.

Chop together and mix with all other ingredients.

Add sea salt and freshly ground black pepper to taste.

Cut French loaf in half lengthwise and remove centre part.

Mix chopped ingredients together with bread that was removed from loaf, with a little olive oil.

Fill the two halves of the bread with mixture and press firmly together.

Packing Instructions
Wrap tightly in foil and refrigerate till picnic time.

Bring knife and slice in half inch pieces at picnic.

SMOKED WILD GOOSE/DUCK 243

Brine
1/4 cup brown sugar
1/4 cup pickling salt
1 cup soya sauce
1 teaspoon onion powder
1 clove garlic, minced
1/2 cup dry sherry
2 Tablespoons grated ginger root
1/2 cup orange juice
1 1/2 cups water

Trim skin and fat (we often use just breasts). Puncture fatty areas with fork. Brine overnight.

Rinse and dry on paper towels for 30 minutes. Smoke for 2 1/2 hours using Cherry or Apple flavor "Chips 'n' Chunks".

Finish cooking in oven at 300ºF one to two hours depending on size of bird.

Smoked meat will appear very dark. It's good hot or cold. Great cold with sauerkraut salad, rye bread and a cold bottle of beer.

SAUERKRAUT PICNIC SALAD 244

28 ounces wine sauerkraut (well drained)
1 cup diced celery
1 cup diced green pepper
1 cup diced Spanish onion
1 can diced pimento (well drained)
1/2 cup white sugar
1/2 cup salad oil
1/2 cup white vinegar

Combine sugar, oil and vinegar. Add to vegetables and marinate overnight.

245　SCOTCH EGG ROLL

Pastry:
1 cup all-purpose flour
pinch of salt
1/4 cup lard
1/4 cup margarine
cold water to mix
a beaten egg to glaze pastry

Filling:
1/2 pound sausage meat
1/4 pound minced beef
1 grated onion
salt and pepper
3 hard boiled eggs

Sift flour and salt in mixing bowl. Rub in the fats and mix the pastry with just enough cold water to a stiff consistency. Mix sausage meat, beef, onion, salt and pepper to taste. Roll out pastry into an 11 x 10 inch rectangle and spread meat filling over centre of pastry, leaving about 1 inch at sides. Lay shelled eggs end to end down centre, then fold one side of pastry over them. Moisten the top edge with water and fold over the other side. Turn ends of pastry up, then roll onto baking tray with joins underneath. Brush roll with beaten egg. Snip top with scissors. Bake at 400°F for 20 minutes, then 350°F for 1 hour more. Cool and slice.

246　WATER CHESTNUT APPETIZERS

1/4 cup soya sauce
1/4 cup Mirin
　　(Sweet Rice cooking wine)
1 can water chestnuts
Bacon

Mix soya sauce and Mirin together, and marinate water chestnuts in mixture for 30 minutes.

Wrap chestnut in 1/2 slice bacon and secure with toothpick which has been soaked with water.

Grill on hibachi or put on rack in pie plate and bake at 400°F for 20 minutes.

Note: You can do this in the morning and return to 350°F oven to warm up just before serving.

This is an old family recipe and should be made a day ahead.

    1 pickled tongue, bought in a plastic bag
    1 teaspoon gelatine
    1/3 can consomme

Simmer tongue in water until very tender — may take 2-3 hours. Skim, drain.

Place tongue in container so that it will unmold attractively. Add gelatine to consomme and heat to dissolve gelatine. Pour over tongue and weight with a brick. Let stand, refrigerated, for at least 12 hours. Unmold on leaf lettuce. Slice thin and serve with hot mustard.

Garnish with cherry tomatoes and fresh dill weed.

SABINA'S BACON AND EGG PIE 248

    8 ounces lean bacon
    4 spring onions
    1 teaspoon butter
    4 eggs
    black pepper
    beaten egg to glaze
    short crust pastry for a double crust pie
        (8" diameter)

Line an 8" pie pan with pastry.

Chop bacon and onions, lightly fry in butter, drain.

Arrange on the pie shell leaving four wells.

Crack eggs into wells, sprinkle with pepper.

Cover pie with top crust.

Brush with beaten egg to glaze.

Make vent in pie crust.

Bake in centre of oven for 40 minutes at 400°F.

Packing Instructions
This is good hot or cold, so just cover with tin foil and take knife and plates for serving.

249   HAM COOKED IN BEER

any size pre-cooked ham
1 or 2 bottles of beer
cloves to garnish
pineapple slices to garnish
maraschino cherries to garnish

Leave rind on ham. Place ham in roasting pan and pour the beer over. Bake for two to three hours at 300°F to 325°F. Baste every fifteen minutes throughout cooking. About the last half hour, remove the rind and score the ham. Decorate with the cloves, pineapple slices and maraschino cherries, and continue basting with the beer.

250   PIERRE'S CHILI

2 — 14 ounce cans tomato sauce
2 — 14 ounce cans chili beans
2 — 14 ounce cans red kidney beans
6 celery stalks, diced
1/2 green pepper
1/4 cup chopped parsley
2 pounds ground beef (medium)
2 cloves garlic, diced
1 red onion, diced
3 Tablespoons chili powder
salt
black pepper
1 teaspoon cayenne
Tabasco sauce
1 bay leaf

Heat tomato sauce, chili beans and kidney beans in saucepan. Saute celery, green pepper and parsley, then add ground beef, garlic, onion, and chili powder. Add to bean mixture. Add all spices. Simmer for one hour.

Packing Instructions
Pierre suggests you pack the chili in an enamel casserole and warm up on picnic stove.

CURRIED APRICOT CORNISH HENS

2 Cornish hens
1 can apricot nectar (10 ounce or pureed apricot)
salt and pepper
curry powder

Wash and clean the hens and with a sharp knife or poultry shears, cut the birds in half. Salt and pepper and in frying pan melt 1 Tablespoon butter and fry till golden brown. Make sure they turn darkish color. Place hens in baking dish or roaster, skin side down. Sprinkle with curry powder generously — rubbing it well into flesh. Pour approximately 3/4 cup apricot nectar over the hens.

Place in 350°F oven and baste 3 or 4 times, turning hens frequently. As baking process continues, the nectar becomes quite thick. Add a touch of cornstarch dissolved in water if too liquid.

Bake 1 1/2 hours or until done. Cool. Carry to picnic in cooler. Serve on a platter surrounded with fresh greens, melon and orange wedges, green pepper rings and devilled eggs. Lemon slices topped with mounds of chutney add the final touch.

LITTLE LAKE BARBECUED RIBS

Serves 6

6 pounds fresh meaty spareribs
3/4 cup catsup
1/2 cup lemon juice
1/2 cup soya sauce
1/2 cup liquid honey

Pre-cook ribs in oven 350°F for 1 hour.

Mix next three ingredients.

Place partially cooked spareribs on hot barbecue grill — brush with sauce, turning several times, about 20 minutes.

Blend honey into remaining sauce. Brush this over ribs to glaze.

Note: Watch this carefully as it burns easily.

253   JEAN'S BEANS

1 pound kidney beans
1 1/2 pounds fresh pork shoulder
1/4 cup salad oil
1/4 teaspoon thyme
1/4 teaspoon garlic salt
1/4 teaspoon allspice
salt and pepper to taste
1 chopped onion, slightly cooked
1 — 20 ounce can tomatoes
1/2 cup molasses
bread crumbs
parsley flakes

Soak beans as directed on package.

Cut meat into 1 inch cubes. While beans are cooking, marinate the meat in oil with seasonings added. Then brown the meat before assembling the casserole.

Put 1/2 of the cooked beans in the bottom of the casserole. Add the browned meat chunks. Add the onion in a layer, the tomatoes, and then the rest of the beans.

Drizzle with molasses. Add a small amount of the cooking water from the beans. Sprinkle with bread crumbs and parsley flakes.

Bake at 350°F, 1 1/2 to 2 hours.

254   MUSTARD BREAD

Slice a loaf of French bread lengthwise.
On *each* half spread generously:
softened butter or margarine
prepared mustard
Next, sprinkle *each* half with
chopped green onion
parsley flakes
sesame seeds
garlic salt

Put the loaf back together and slice into 1 inch chunks.

Wrap in foil (or in a plastic bag if you intend to heat in microwave) and heat before serving.

This loaf freezes very well and is great for barbecues, picnics, and taking to the ski hill.

1 pound ground beef
2 onions, chopped
2 cloves garlic
1 large can tomatoes with juice
freshly ground pepper to taste
2 teaspoons salt
2 Tablespoons chili powder
1 cup kernel corn
1/2 cup chopped green pepper
3/4 cup corn meal
1 Tablespoon flour
1 Tablespoon sugar
1 1/2 teaspoons baking powder
1 beaten egg
1/3 cup milk
1 Tablespoon cooking oil

Preheat oven to 425ºF.

Saute in lightly greased pan, ground beef and chopped onion. Cook till ground beef is brown and onion translucent. Add garlic, tomatoes, pepper, salt, chili, kernel corn and green pepper and simmer for 15 minutes.

Meanwhile, sift and mix together cornmeal, flour, sugar and baking powder, and moisten with egg and milk. Mix lightly and fold in oil.

Place meat mixture in a greased 2 quart stoneware casserole and cover with the corn bread topping. (The topping disappears but rises to form a good layer of corn bread).

Place in oven and bake 20-25 minutes or until corn bread is brown.

CHICKEN ROLL KALEIDOSCOPE

*Serves
6-8*

2 1/2 pounds boned whole chicken
1/4 cup minced parsley
1 teaspoon oregano
1/4 teaspoon pepper
10 soft oil-cured olives, pitted
   and sliced
1/4 pound salami, thinly sliced
3 hard boiled eggs, halved crosswise
1/2 teaspoon salt
bacon strips

Have butcher bone chicken and cut it down the back so there is one large unbroken piece of meat.

Spread chicken skin side down on wax paper and fold in the meat from the legs (we turned the legs inside out), spreading it over any loose skin and forming as even a layer of meat as possible.

Sprinkle with salt and pepper, cover with wax paper, and pound with a meat cleaver until uniform in thickness. Remove wax paper.

In small bowl, combine parsley, oregano and pepper.

Sprinkle 1/2 of this mixture over chicken, then spread olives over mixture.

Arrange salami over olives and sprinkle salami with remaining parsley.

Arrange eggs along centre of chicken (lengthwise).

Fold in ends of chicken and beginning with one of the long sides, roll meat tightly around eggs. Tie roll with string at 1" intervals, making sure skin encloses all of filling.

Sprinkle roll with oregano, salt and pepper and cover top with bacon strips.

Place roll seam-side down in a roasting pan and bake in a moderate oven 350°F basting several times for 50 minutes.

Remove bacon strips and return the chicken roll to a 425°F oven for 10-15 minutes more, till lightly browned.

Cool to room temperature. Chill overnight.

Slice roll into 3/4" slices and leave at room temperature for about 1 hour.

Serve on a platter garnished with oil-cured black olives and tomato wedges.

QUICK ANISE BREAD

3 cups unbleached flour
1 cup wheat germ
1/2 cup brown sugar
1 Tablespoon baking powder
1 teaspoon salt
2 Tablespoons anise seeds
1 1/2 cups milk
2 eggs
2 Tablespoons oil
dash vanilla
dash lemon juice

Preheat oven to 350°F.

Grease 9" round pan.

Mix all ingredients together. It makes a gooey batter.

Dampen hands with water and pat into round pan.

Bake 40-45 minutes.

Optional: You can add 1/2 cup currants or 1/2 cup raisins.

QUICK BRAN LOAF

2 cups flour
1 teaspoon salt
4 teaspoons baking powder
1/2 cup dark brown sugar
1 1/2 cups bran
1 egg
1 cup milk

Sift and measure flour, add salt and baking powder and sift again. Blend in sugar and bran. Make a well in the centre and add egg beaten with milk. Stir gently — just to moisten dry ingredients.

Spoon into greased loaf pan.

Bake at 325°F for one hour or until done.

Serve with wine cured Cheddar and September's first apples.

STEPHEN BEST'S BEST RAISIN BREAD

1/2 cup lukewarm water
1 teaspoon sugar
1 package active dry yeast
1 Tablespoon salt
2 Tablespoons sugar
2 Tablespoons butter
1 cup boiling water
1 cup cold milk
2 eggs
1 cup bran
5-6 cups whole wheat flour
2 cups chopped raisins

Dissolve 1 teaspoon sugar in 1/2 cup lukewarm water. Sprinkle yeast over top and let stand 10 minutes.

Fill a shallow roasting pan with hot water and place it on the lower rack of oven.

Mix salt, sugar and butter into 1 cup boiling water and then add 1 cup cold milk and eggs.

In a large bowl, combine this mixture with 1 cup whole wheat flour and add the yeast mixture to this.

Add 1 cup bran and mix well.

Add 3 cups flour and mix well after each cup.

Chop 2 cups of raisins with a wet knife and add to bread.

Add 1 to 2 more cups of flour, using only enough flour so that the bread can be kneaded without sticking to the hands.

Butter hands well and knead the bread for about 5 minutes.

Butter a large bowl. Form the bread into one large loaf and place it in the bowl.

Place on top rack of oven and leave till doubled in bulk, about 1 hour, and remove.

Replace the water in pan with hot water again.

Punch down bread, cover with tea towel and let rest for 10 minutes.

Grease 2 loaf pans with butter.

Place bread on floured surface and knead for almost ten minutes.

(continued)

Cut in half. Form each half into a loaf and place in pans.

Put in oven for 50 minutes to double in bulk. Leave bread in oven and turn it on to 350°F.

Bake for 1 hour.

Take bread out of pans and place on sides covered with tea towel to cool.

Makes two loaves.

SPICY APPLE MUFFINS 260

Part I
2 cups whole wheat flour
1/4 cup wheat germ
2 teaspoons baking soda
1 teaspoon salt
1 teaspoon cinnamon
1/2 teaspoon nutmeg
3/4 cup chopped walnuts
4 large apples

Part II
2 eggs
1 cup white sugar
1 cup brown sugar
1/2 cup oil
1 teaspoon vanilla

Part I
Mix the dry ingredients together.

Peel and coarsely chop apples and mix into dry ingredients.

Part II
Mix well in large bowl. Add the apple mixture to the wet ingredients and stir together with a wooden spoon. This is a very stiff batter.

Pack into large greased and floured muffin tins.

Bake at 350°F until firm to touch.

Note: This batter may be packed into a greased 9" x 13" pan and baked at 350°F for about 50 minutes.

WELSH CAKES

3 cups sifted flour
1 1/2 teaspoons baking powder
1/2 teaspoon soda
1 teaspoon salt
1/2 cup berry sugar
1 teaspoon nutmeg
1/4 teaspoon mace
1 cup shortening
2 eggs, beaten
4 Tablespoons milk
3/4 cup washed currants
1/4 cup mixed peel

Sift the dry ingredients together.

Using a pastry blender, cut in the shortening.

Add the beaten eggs combined with milk.

Blend in currants and peel.

Roll dough to 1/2" thickness. Cut into 2" rounds.

Bake in an electric frying pan at 300°F about 10 minutes on each side.

Store in airtight cookie container.

Indispensable for campers, hikers, tea party-ers and lazy breakfasters. They are solid, easy to pack and very satisfying.

SASKATOON BERRY PIE

1 cup diced rhubarb
3 cups saskatoon berries
1/4 teaspoon cinnamon
1/4 teaspoon ginger
1/2 cup white sugar
1 Tablespoon minute tapioca
1 Tablespoon lemon juice
2 teaspoons cornstarch
1/4 cup water
1 — 9" pie shell, baked

Stew rhubarb in 1 Tablespoon water and sweeten to taste.

Add cinnamon and ginger, saskatoon berries, sugar, tapioca and lemon juice in saucepan. Let stand for 1/2 hour.

Brush the inside of baked pie shell with melted butter.

Mix cornstarch and water and add to berry mixture. Place on medium heat and stir until berries are soft.

Cool slightly and pour into pie shell.

Decorate with whipped cream.

GRAND MARNIER SAUCE

Serves 10

5 egg yolks
1/2 cup plus 2 Tablespoons sugar
1/4 cup Grand Marnier
1 cup heavy cream

Add the yolks and half a cup of sugar to a 2 quart mixing bowl that will rest snugly on top of a slightly larger saucepan. Add about 2 inches of water to saucepan and bring to a boil. Beat egg yolks with a wire whisk or portable electric beater, making sure you scrape around the inside bottom of the bowl with the beater. Place the mixing bowl in the saucepan and do not allow bowl to touch water. Continue beating for 10 minutes or so until yolks are quite thick and pale yellow.

Remove bowl from saucepan and stir in half the Grand Marnier, allow sauce to cool, then refrigerate until thoroughly cold. Beat the cream with 2 Tablespoons sugar until it is almost, but not quite, stiff. Fold cream into sauce and stir in remaining Grand Marnier.

Use as a dip for any fruit. Great with strawberries.

CHOCOLATE CAKE — WEARY WILLIE —

No picnic can be without one.

> 2 squares unsweetened chocolate
> 2 Tablespoons butter
> 1 cup flour
> 1 cup sugar
> 1 1/2 teaspoons baking powder
> 1 egg — in a measuring cup add milk
>   to 1 cup level
> 1 teaspoon vanilla

Melt chocolate and butter. Sift flour, baking powder and sugar into a mixing bowl. Beat in milk and egg and melted chocolate. Blend well. Pour into greased and floured 8" x 8" pan. Bake 350°F 35 minutes or until cake tests done.

Cool and frost with:

> *Chocolate Butter Icing*
> 1 3/4 cups icing sugar
> 1/4 cup cocoa
> 4 teaspoons butter
> 1/2 teaspoon vinegar
> 1/2 Tablespoon vanilla

A little cream to make it spreading consistency. Beat well. Cut cake in 16 pieces.

Don't double or freeze. This should be eaten as soon as it is frosted as it is a light, fresh chocolate cake with a creamy frosting. Wonderful with a tall glass of cold milk, wonderful any way!

BOILED RAISIN COOKIES   265

1 1/2 cups raisins
1 1/2 cups water

Cook together in saucepan until water is all gone. Cool.

3 cups flour
1 teaspoon soda
1 teaspoon baking powder
1 teaspoon cinnamon
1 teaspoon salt
1 cup shortening
1 1/4 cups brown sugar
2 eggs
1 cup walnuts

Sift flour with soda, baking powder, cinnamon and salt. Cream shortening and sugar. Add eggs, beating well. Add dry ingredients alternately with raisins. Add walnuts. Drop by teaspoon onto greased baking sheet. Bake 350°F for 10-12 minutes, or until set and browned.

SPECIALS   266

1 cup brown sugar
1/2 cup melted butter
1 Tablespoon molasses
1/4 cup chocolate chips
1/4 cup chopped walnuts
2 cups rolled oats
1 teaspoon baking powder

Cream sugar, butter and molasses. Stir in remaining ingredients.

Press into a greased 7" x 11" or 8" square pan. Put in oven for approximately 15 minutes at 350°F.

Cut into fingers while still warm.

'COMIN' THROUGH THE RYE' CAKE

A delicious torte that must be made ahead and allowed to ripen with the filling. Any sponge or layer cake may be used instead of the orange cake given.

Buttermilk Orange Cake
1 cup butter
2 cups sugar
5 eggs
2 oranges, rind grated
3 Tablespons orange juice
3 cups sifted flour
1 teaspoon soda
1/2 teaspoon salt
1 cup buttermilk

Butter a 10" tube pan. Line bottom with waxed paper, also lightly greased.

Cream butter and sugar. Add eggs one at a time and beat well for three minutes.

Combine sifted flour, soda and salt. On lowest speed add dry ingredients alternating with buttermilk, beating only until smooth.

Stir in juice and rind. Pour into pan. Bake at least one hour at 350°F until cake tests done.

When cool cut into 3 or 4 layers.

Rye Filling
(keeps several weeks in refrigerator)
1/2 cup butter
3/4 cup sugar
6 egg yolks
1/2 teaspoon salt
1/4 cup rye or bourbon
3/4 cup coconut
3/4 cup sliced maraschino cherries
3/4 cup pecans
3/4 cup raisins

(continued)

Melt butter and sugar. Beat in yolks and return to simmer. Mixture will thicken and coat a spoon. Remove from heat and stir in remaining ingredients. Fill layers and wrap cake tightly in saran at least one day. Top with sweetened whipped cream on same day as serving.

CLOVE CAKE 268

1 cup butter or margarine
2 1/4 cups sugar
5 eggs
3 cups flour
1 Tablespoon cloves
1 Tablespoon cinnamon
1/4 teaspoon salt
1 cup sour milk
1 teaspoon baking soda

Cream butter and sugar until light. Add eggs, one at a time, beating after each. Sift together dry ingredients, add alternately with sour milk.

Bake in greased and floured 10" tube pan, 350°F for 55-65 minutes. Let cool for 20 minutes. Remove from pan. When cool frost with vanilla butter frosting. Decorate top with a row of whole walnut halves around edge.

SKI COUNTRY COFFEE 269

Serves 8

2 cups strong coffee
(preferably prepared from dark roast)
1/4 cup demerara sugar
2 ounces bittersweet chocolate
1/4 teaspoon cinnamon
2 1/2 cups hot milk
1/3 cup rum or brandy
whipping cream
cinnamon
grated chocolate

Combine coffee, sugar, chocolate and cinnamon.

Heat until chocolate melts.

Heat the milk in a heavy saucepan.

Pour the hot coffee into the milk and whip until frothy. Add the rum.

Pour into warmed mugs, top with lots of whipped cream, and a dash of cinnamon and chocolate.

270 THELMA'S UNBEATABLE FUDGE

1 cup walnuts
1 cup semi-sweet chocolate chips
1/2 teaspoon vanilla
1/2 cup butter cut in small chunks

12 marshmallows (large size)
1 small can Alpha milk (6 ounces)
2 cups white sugar

Mix first four ingredients in large bowl. Set aside. Place marshmallows, milk and sugar in a heavy saucepan and bring to a boil slowly. Continue to simmer for 12-15 minutes stirring constantly. Pour over ingredients in bowl, melting butter in the process. Pour into greased 8" square pan. Cool and cut in squares.

271 ORANGES IN CARAMEL

8 large oranges (thin skinned
are the best)

Thinly pare the skin from one orange using a potato peeler. Julienne into fine strips. Cook 5 minutes in boiling water, then dry.

Peel the oranges, including all the pith, then slice and reshape orange by inserting toothpick through all segments.

Caramel
1 cup sugar
1/2 cup water
1/4 cup cointreau, or any other orange-
based liqueur
1/2 cup warm water

Melt sugar in heavy saucepan, then bring to a boil and boil steadily without stirring. Keep heat low while melting sugar and then let it boil. Cook to rich brown caramel. Watch carefully at end as it turns brown rather quickly. Add warm water and return to heat till caramel is melted. Add cointreau. Add julienned peel and pour over oranges. Refrigerate.

THE GARDEN ROOM'S WILD RICE SOUP 272

Serves 6

1 small onion, finely chopped
2 Tablespoons butter
1/2 pound mushrooms, thinly sliced
1/2 cup celery, thinly sliced
1/4 cup flour
4 cups chicken stock, hot
1 cup wild rice, cooked
1/4 teaspoon salt
1/4 teaspoon dry mustard
1/4 teaspoon curry powder
1/8 teaspoon white pepper
1 cup light cream
1/2 cup dry sherry
2 Tablespoons parsley, finely chopped

In a large, heavy saucepan saute onions in butter. Add mushrooms and celery and cook for 2 minutes. Add flour and stir well. Gradually add hot broth, stirring until it thickens. Stir in rice, salt, curry powder, pepper, dry mustard. Simmer gently, do not boil. Add cream and sherry. Serve immediately with a sprinkle of parsley.

CHILLED AVOCADO AND CONSOMMÉ 273

avocado
mayonnaise
consommé
curry powder

In small individual parfait glasses or soufflé cups, scoop some avocado. Spread mayonnaise on top. Smooth top. Warm consommé a little. Sprinkle a dash of curry powder over mayonnaise and cover very carefully with a little consommé.

Chill until gelled. Add more consommé to make a thick layer.

Set in refrigerator. Decorate with a little parsley.

Serve with a good brown bread and unsalted butter.

A delicious starting course.

CREME PALAHNA

Serves 4-6

1 cup cream
1/2 cup milk
1/2 cup sugar
dash of salt
1 envelope unflavored gelatine
1 cup sour cream
1/2 teaspoon almond extract or
    2 Tablespoons brandy
saskatoons or wild blueberries,
    sweetened with maple syrup

Combine first four ingredients in a saucepan and cook ov
low heat, stirring until sugar is dissolved. Remove from hea
Soften gelatine in 1/4 cup cold water and stir into crea
mixture. When gelatine is completely dissolved, beat in th
sour cream with a hand beater only until thoroughly blende
and smooth.

Blend in flavorings.

Pour into individual serving dishes.

Chill until firm.

Serve with the berries.

This dessert is all the more satisfying for its simplicity. Th
dessert honors a grandmother who, although she nev
made it, did pick a lot of saskatoons in her time. To yo
Palahna!

Yields: 60

3 ounces fresh Fleischmann's Yeast*
   or 3 envelopes of dry yeast
1/2 cup sugar
1 cup warm water
3 cups warm water
1 cup melted butter or margarine
1 cup milk powder
1/2 cup sugar
1 Tablespoon salt
1 1/2 cups mashed potatoes
4 eggs, lightly beaten
1 teaspoon baking powder
15 cups all-purpose flour (more or less)

In a small bowl combine 1/2 cup sugar and yeast with 1 cup warm water and set aside until yeast bubbles, about 10 minutes.

In a very large bowl combine 3 cups warm water, 1 cup milk powder, melted butter, 1/2 cup sugar, salt, mashed potatoes, eggs and 2 cups of the flour with 1 teaspoon baking powder.

Beat until smooth.

Add softened yeast and stir.

Gradually add more flour until dough is stiff and not sticky. Grease hands with oil, round dough in a ball and knead until smooth and elastic, about 5 minutes.

Grease, cover with a cloth and place in warm place until double in size, about 1 hour.

Punch down. Form into buns to fit in muffin pans (Crescent rolls, Parkerhouse rolls, Clover Leaf rolls or any shape you like). Allow to rise again.

Brush top of buns with melted butter or margarine.

Bake in 350ºF oven for 20 minutes or until golden brown.

*Fresh Fleischmann's Yeast can be bought at any bakery shop by the pound. Divide pound into 5 parts, wrap in foil and freeze for future use.

ROAST WILD GOOSE WITH CUMBERLAND SAUCE

1 wild goose
salt
pepper
1 large onion
10 juniper berries

Wash and dry goose. Sprinkle salt and pepper inside and out. Peel onion, remove centre part and fill with juniper berries. Place onion in cavity of goose, place goose *breast side down* on rack in roasting pan.

Cover bottom of pan with cold water. Place in 325ºF oven for 1 hour, adding cold water as it evaporates. Turn and roast breast side up for 45 minutes more, lowering oven temperature to 300ºF. *Remove onion from cavity.

Transfer goose to another pan and return to oven for 20 minutes more.

Scrape bottom of roaster to loosen browned bits (save to use with sauce).

*To prepare ahead: Prepare bird up to * Remove from oven. Cool until you can handle and take breast meat off bones without breaking meat. Also remove legs.

Wrap each breast and leg with a little of the juice from the roaster pan separately in foil.

At this point, the meat can be held until you are ready for dinner. 30 minutes before you are ready to eat it, place in preheated oven at 300ºF for 20 minutes. Goose should be served pink. Slice breasts very thinly and pour Cumberland Sauce over goose.

CUMBERLAND SAUCE 277

2 slices fresh ginger, julienned
1 orange
1 cup Madeira or Port wine
1 Tablespoon lemon juice
1/2 cup red currant jelly or
    crab apple jelly
browned bits from roaster

Peel the orange, being careful not to include the white pith.

Cut peeling into very fine slivers.

Cook ginger and orange rind with wine and browned bits until reduced by 1/3.

Add juice of the orange and lemon juice and jelly.

Stir until jelly is melted.

CHEN'S POCKETS 278

1 pound package egg roll wraps*
oil for deep fat frying

Thaw wraps, if frozen. Heat oil to 375ºF. Gently put one roll wrap at a time on top of oil. Press down into hot oil with a soup ladle so that wrap comes up around bowl of ladle. Fry until golden and crisp. Remove and drain inverted on paper towelling. Store in a cool place, tightly covered. At serving time, mound high in a wicker basket. Use as pockets to fill with any hot or cold savory creamed filling.

*They come 5" by 5" in which case use them whole, but for a luncheon use 7" by 7" ones — cut in quarters. Used whole equals at least 25 pockets per package.

279   WILD RICE CASSEROLE

Serves
8-10

2 cups wild rice
1/2 cup butter
1 cup whole blanched almonds
4 green onions, finely chopped
2 medium carrots, shredded
3 cans consomme

Saute rice in butter. Remove rice to a greased casserole, add next three ingredients and saute until onion is tender, and almonds slightly browned. Add to casserole along with consomme. This must stand a while. Either combine ingredients in the morning, and keep in refrigerator until dinner or overnight, at which time bake 350ºF for 2 hours, uncovered,

Or

Can be assembled and baked along with Pork Medallions — at 250ºF for 5 hours — water may be added as needed as rice cooks.

280   HONEYED WILD DUCK

2 wild ducks — cut in half
2 Tablespoons soya sauce
1 Tablespoon sugar
4 Tablespoons honey
5 Tablespoons dry sherry

Combine soya sauce, sugar, honey and sherry. Rub outside of ducks with this mixture and let stand in refrigerator for 3 hours turning twice. Rub inside of duck with salt and place in pan. Pour soya mixture over and broil till medium rare.*

*Can Also Be Barbecued — basting duck with soya mixture.

Duck meat should be juicy — meaning medium rare. Those who claim they don't like wild duck probably have never tasted a duck cooked this way.

LEMON CHIFFON RING

4 teaspoons gelatine
1/2 cup cold water
2/3 cup sugar
2/3 cup fresh lemon juice
6 eggs, separated
2 teaspoons grated lemon rind
1/3 cup sugar

Soften gelatine in cold water. Mix sugar and lemon juice. Beat egg yolks until thick and lemon colored, and mix into sugar and lemon juice. Cook in top of double boiler until mixture coats a spoon. Remove from heat, add gelatine and dissolve. Add grated lemon rind. Chill until mixture begins to thicken. Beat egg whites stiff. Add sugar gradually. Fold into thickening mixture. Pour into large ring mold and chill until set — about three hours. Unmold and serve with fresh strawberries, mint leaves, orange sections.

CANDIED ORANGE RIND

2 large oranges
3/4 cup sugar
1/4 cup water
1 Tablespoon white corn syrup
sugar

Remove peel from oranges, slice into narrow strips.

Place peel in saucepan with cold water to cover. Simmer until orange strips are tender, 8-10 minutes.

Drain, set aside.

Combine sugar, water and corn syrup in saucepan, cook until sugar is dissolved. Add orange slivers, simmer until syrup is thick, 25 minutes.

Drain peel and place on wire cake racks to dry, 2 hours.

Roll in sugar. If desired, dip one end of each strip in melted semi-sweet chocolate.

Makes about 2 cups.

Stores well in tightly covered jar in refrigerator. Super emergency-shelf item. Serve with espresso instead of dessert.

283 THE BEST CHOCOLATE SAUCE IN ALL THE WORLD

2 squares unsweetened chocolate
2 Tablespoons butter
2/3 cup boiling water
2 cups sugar
4 Tablespoons white corn syrup
1 teaspoon vanilla
salt

Melt chocolate and butter in saucepan. Add boiling water very slowly. Gradually bring to the boil. Add sugar, salt and syrup. Boil gently for 5 minutes. Cover. Cool. Add vanilla.

Serve warm over ice cream.

284 JUBILEE RUM MOUSSE

Serves 4-6

1 Tablespoon gelatine
1/4 cup cold water
4 eggs, separated
1 cup sugar
1/2 cup half and half cream
8 Tablespoons dark rum
1/2 pint whipping cream, whipped
dash nutmeg
1 bar sweet chocolate, about 2
    ounces, grated

Soak gelatine in the water for 10 minutes.

Beat egg yolks and sugar well. Add half and half cream. Cook in double boiler, stirring until mixture thickens and is slightly creamy.

Add soaked gelatine to hot mixture and stir until dissolved. Cool until partially set. Fold in rum, stiffly beaten egg whites and whipped cream. Mound into souffle dish (2 quart). Garnish with nutmeg and a bar of grated sweet chocolate.

Chill for 2-3 hours or overnight.

CHOCOLATE ROLL

There is no flour in this recipe.

Serves 8

6 eggs, separated
1/2 cup plus 2 Tablespoons sugar
6 Tablespoons cocoa
1 teaspoon vanilla
1/2 teaspoon almond extract

Beat egg yolks until lemon colored and very fluffy. Gradually beat in sugar and flavorings. Stir in cocoa then fold mixture into stiffly beaten egg whites. Pour into jelly roll pan which has been greased and lined with wax paper.

Bake 350°F — 25 minutes or until done.

Turn out immediately onto towel that has been dusted with icing sugar. Peel off wax paper and trim any crisp edges. Roll firmly starting at shorter edge rolling towel right along with it. When cool, unroll gently and fill with Charlotte Russe, then roll up again. Frost with rich dark chocolate frosting. May be frozen.

Charlotte Russe Filling
1/2 Tablespoon gelatine
1/8 cup cold water
1/8 cup boiling water
1/2 cup sugar
1 cup whipping cream
1 teaspoon vanilla

Soak gelatine in cold water for 3 minutes. Dissolve softened gelatine and sugar in boiling water. Cool a little. Add vanilla. Whip cream until it begins to thicken. Gradually drip in gelatine mixture. Beat until firm peaks form.

286 PUMPKIN CHEESE CAKE

Serves 16

Crust:

1 1/2 cups gingersnap cookie crumbs
1/3 cup butter

Combine. Line bottom of spring form pan. Bake 350ºF for 10 minutes.

Filling:

6 eggs
1 pound cream cheese
1 — 14 ounce can pumpkin
1 teaspoon cinnamon
1/2 teaspoon each cloves, nutmeg,
    ginger, and salt
2/3 cup evaporated milk or cream
3/4 cup sugar

In a food processor or mixer beat all ingredients for the filling till well blended. Pour into baked crust. Bake 350ºF for 1 hour. Remove from oven. Spread glaze over. Increase heat to 450ºF. Bake 5 minutes more.

Glaze:

Mix 1 cup sour cream with 1/4 cup brown sugar.

Note: Let stand at least overnight. Pipe sweetened whipped cream around edge.

287 CRÈME BRÛLÉE COINTREAU

Serves 8

1 quart whipping cream
1 vanilla bean*
4 Tablespoons sugar
8 egg yolks
dash salt
1 cup light brown sugar
Cointreau (if desired)

Scald cream with vanilla bean. Add sugar and stir to dissolve. Beat egg yolks with salt and stir in hot cream mixture. Strain mixture into 8 individual souffle dishes. Place dishes in pan of hot water in 350ºF oven for 35 minutes or until knife inserted in center comes out clean. Remove pans from hot water. Cool. Refrigerate until very cold or overnight.

(continued)

Near serving time — Sieve brown sugar. Smooth a layer over each custard (about 1/4" thick) The top must be smooth. Broil about 4-5 inches from broiler until top is caramelized (watch carefully). Dishes may be ready at different times. Cool before serving.

At serving time — crack caramel with a spoon — place 1/2 teaspoon of Cointreau in the crack.

*Vanilla bean may be used, rinsed in water, dried, rolled in sugar and stored for use again.

CHOCOLATE POPPY SEED TORTE 288

Serves 12

1/2 cup butter
3/4 cup sugar
6 egg yolks (large)
1 cup cocoa
6 Tablespoons oil
1 teaspoon vanilla
6 egg whites
1/4 teaspoon cream of tartar
1/2 cup finely ground poppy seeds
2 Tablespoons graham cracker crumbs

Grease a 10" spring form pan.

Preheat oven to 350ºF.

Cream butter and sugar. Add egg yolks and beat well.

Mix cocoa and oil. Stir in vanilla. Add to creamed mixture along with poppy seeds that have been ground well in a blender or food processor. Beat egg whites with cream of tartar to fairly stiff peaks. Pour chocolate mixture over beaten egg whites, folding well with spatula.

Sprinkle crumbs over entire surface and fold in gently.

Bake 1 hour at 350ºF.

Let stand at least 1 day before serving. Frost with sweetened whipped cream.

PINEAPPLE DELIGHT

Serves
10-12

Grease two 8" round pans and dust with flour.
Preheat oven to 350ºF.

Mix I

Combine the following ingredients in a bowl and beat with mixer until smooth.

4 egg yolks
1/2 cup flour
1 teaspoon baking powder
4 Tablespoons milk
1/2 cup shortening
1/2 cup sugar

Spread in prepared pans. This is a thin layer.

Mix II

4 egg whites
3/4 cup sugar
1 teaspoon vanilla
3/4 cup walnuts, finely chopped

Beat egg whites until stiff. Gradually add sugar. Fold in vanilla and walnuts. Spread Mix II over Mix I in both pans. Bake at 350ºF for 1/2 hour.

Cool.

Place one layer on plate, egg whites down. Fill with a mixture of

1 cup whipped cream
2 Tablespoons powdered sugar
1 can crushed pineapple (well drained)

(sliced, drained strawberries may be substituted for pineapple)

Top with other layer and garnish with whipped cream and fruit or toasted almonds.

COINTREAU CHEESE CAKE   290

Serves
15-20

Crust:
1 package thin chocolate wafers
1/3 cup butter, melted

Crush wafers, blend in melted butter.

Pat into 9" x 13" cake pan or large springform pan.

Filling:
rind of one large orange
2 cups berry sugar
2/3 cup *cold* butter
2 — 8 ounce packages cold cream cheese
1 envelope gelatine
1/4 cup water
2/3 cup Cointreau
1 2/3 cups whipping cream

Cream butter and cream cheese, add rind and sugar. Beat until light and fluffy. Soften gelatine in water, then dissolve over medium heat. Stir in Cointreau. Cool. Blend into orange mixture. Whip cream, fold in. Pour over chocolate crust. Refrigerate overnight. Must be chilled to cut well. Garnish with sweetened whipped cream and a sliver of candied orange rind.

Freezes beautifully.

TIA MARIA TORTE   291

1 pound package Dad's Chocolate
    Chip Cookies
1/3 cup Tia Maria
1/3 cup milk
1 pint whipping cream, whipped
chocolate chips

Butter springform pan. Dip each cookie in Tia Maria, mixed with milk. Do not soak. Layer cookies with unsweetened whipped cream. Sprinkle with chocolate chips.

Refrigerate overnight.

The Recipe Donors

*The Edmonton Arts Cookbook Society thanks all who
have so generously shared so many favorite recipes.
We regret not having the space to use every one.*

Doug Abrams
Giuseppe G. Albi
Barbara Allen
Margaret Andrekson
Dorothy Astle
Ann Austin

Diana Bacon
Chris and Wilf Backhaus
Irma Backhaus
Betty Jean Baldwin
Bobbie Baldwin
Kathy Ball
Tommy Banks
Jean Bell
Janet Bentley
Annabel Berretti
Stephen Best
Agnes Birss
Audrey Bishop
Suzanne Blackner
Con Boland
Betty Bond
Enid and George Botchett
Elizabeth Brandt
Paddy Brine
Wendy Bryan
Betty Jean Buchanan
Helen Buck
June Bulat

Betty Carlson
Dorothy Cameron
Molly Carter
Shelagh Carver
John Charles
Jacqueline Charlesworth
Bruno Chicchini
Eleanor Clark
Nancy Clarke
Joyce Cook
Marg Cormack

Clari Cowan
Doreen Crone-Findlay

Michele Deland
Don Delaney
Joan Dickins
Keith Digby
Berenice Dunsworth
Trudy Dvorkin

Svea Eklot
Jean Ensell
Carole Ernst Eder
Charlotte Evans
Sylvia Ewanchuk

Sheila Fenton
Terry Fenton
Paddy Fernandez-Davila
Tilly Fischer
Mary Fitzgerald
Edythe Florence
Jean Forest
Darlene Forrester
Francesco Hair Design
Jean Fraser
Phyllis J. Freeman
Roz Friedman

Betty Gaetz
Angela Gann
Merrilyn Gann
Christopher Gaze
Joshua Gaze
Frances Geddes
Rae Geddes
Lorraine Gillespie
Hertha Giroux
Richard Gishler
Michelle Goodger
Doug Graham
Warren Graves

Ruth Grundy
Pierre Guy

Lelia Hamilton
Joyce Harries
Laurie Harrison
Doug Haynes
Eirene Hebb
Maureen Hemingway
Rosemary Hoare
Janice Hodgson
Rob Hood
Helen Hope
Barbara Horowitz
Ruth Huang
Barbara Hunt
Elizabeth Hyde

Jean Irving

Joan Jackson
Pearl Jin
Jeanne Johnston
Mary Judge
John and Donna Juliani

Kee Lo, Moveable Fea
Barbara Kelly
Maryalice Kennedy
John King
Claire Kirkland
Irene Klar
Sally Knowlton
Myrna Kostash
M. Krausert
Brenda Kravic
Barbara Kyle

Anita Lavallee
Roy Leadbeater
Nancy Lieberman
Kathie Leitch

Hilda Lilly
Carol Lockwood
Marlie Lockerbie
Patsy Lord
Jeanne Lougheed
David L. Lovett
Judy Lowery
Agnes Lynch
Allan Lysell

Dorothea Macdonnell
Mary Maclean
Marlene Maitell
Thelma Manarey
Ruth Mansfield
Colleen Manuel
Joan Manuel
Doreen Mason
Peggy Matheson
Jeanne Mathieson
Elizabeth McBride
Lois McCalla
Peter McCoppin
Lorraine McDonald
Betty McDonough
Barbara McGregor
Barbara McLeod
Ellen McNerny
Eva Milanson
Gwen Molnar
Margaret Morris
Norma Morrison
Joyce Mustard

Affy Newson
Mary Nursall

Louella Oeste
Seka Owen

Joyce Pearson
Eva Paletz
Queenie Palmer
Mary Pardee
Denny Parlee
Bobbie Patrick
Tom Peacocke
Kay Pearson
Ethel Peet

Linda Peet
Sheila Peterson
Jackie Phillips
Barbara Poole
Grazia Poretti
Helen Potter
Helen Primrose

Michel Rahn
Marion Ramsay
Janice Reilly
Cathy Rogers
Bea Rolf
Georgia Ross

Lorna Savok
Helen Schlosser
Patricia Schlosser
Judith and Mark Schoenberg
Brownie Scott
Carol Selfridge
Richard Selfridge
Edith Sellers
Sandra Shaul

Dodie Sherbaniuk
Marion Shipley
Bill Slavik
Isabel Smith
Edna Snell
Marnie Sproule
Barbara Stokoe
Strawberry Cafe — Monica Guilini and
Strawberry Cafe — Arden Schlosser
Jane Sturgeon
Scott Swan
Valerie Swann
Ruby Swekla

Mary Tasopulos
Audrey Taylor
Eileen Taylor
Maggi Taylor
Telegraph House, Nova Scotia
Agnes Thompson
Shirley Thompson
Kathryn Tulk
Sandy Turnbull
Sydney Turner

Evelyn Underhill

Vicki Vaitkunus
Lois Verchomin

Hazel Walker
Jean Ward
Brian Webb
Elizabeth Welsh
Monica Wilson
Harriett Winspear
Pat Wood
Verlie Wood

Irma Young

METRIC CONVERSION

OVEN TEMPERATURES

	Fahrenheit	Celsius
Very slow	250°-275°	121°-135°
Slow	300°-325°	149°-163°
Moderate	350°-375°	177°-191°
Hot	400°-425°	204°-218°
Very Hot	450°-475°	232°-246°
Extremely Hot	500°-525°	260°-274°

COOKING MEASUREMENTS

Imperial Measure	Approximate Metric Measure	
¼ teaspoon	1.25	millilitres
½ teaspoon	2.5	millilitres
1 teaspoon	5	millilitres
1 Tablespoon	15	millilitres
1 fluid ounce	30	millilitres
1 cup	250	millilitres
3/4 cup	175	millilitres
2/3 cup	150	millilitres
1/2 cup	125	millilitres
1/3 cup	75	millilitres
1/4 cup	50	millilitres

PAN MEASUREMENTS

Imperial	Metric
8" x 8"	20 cm x 20 cm
9" x 9"	22 cm x 22 cm
9" x 13"	22 cm x 33 cm

MASS

2 pounds is slightly less than	1 kg
1 ounce is approximately	30 g

LENGTH

½ inch is slightly more than	1 cm
2 inches is approximately	5 cm

INDEX

A

197

D

M

N

O

P

Q

R

S

Sabina's Bacon & Egg Pie 248

SALADS:
Al Fresco 236
Asparagus Vinaigrette 112
Bishop's 5
Cantaloupe and Blackberry 111
Cucumber, Crab 232
Fruit Cheese Mold 9
German Potato 228
Good Lady Chicken 7
Grapefruit Cucumber Mold 8
Holly Wreath 63
Orange, Onion 231
Papaya 110
Sauerkráut 244
Schnippled Bean 4
Spinach 233
Tabbouleh 241
Tomato 234
Zucchini 3
Zucchini Slaw 229

SANDWICH FILLINGS:
Chicken or Tuna Rounds 182
Smoked Salmon Fingers 181
Watercress Sandwiches 183
Saskatoon Berry Pie 262

SAUCES:
MAIN COURSE:
Cumberland 277
Curried Fruit Bake 27
English Mustard 29
Marinated Onions with Sour Cream 6
Mustard 58
Prezzemolo 127

DESSERT:
Apples Pronto 148
Best Chocolate 283
Grand Marnier 263
September 149
Saucy Baked Beans 42
Sauerkraut Salad 244
Savoury French Loaf 242
Scalloped Oysters 166
Scallops St. Georges 145
Scotch Egg Roll 245
Scottish Dressing for Turkey 56
Schnippled Bean Salad 4

SEAFOOD, FISH: (also see appetizers and soups)
Avocado Crepes with Crab Filling 22
Baked Whole Salmon or Arctic Char 33
Casserole from the Sea 144
Crepes with Shrimp Filling 25
Linguine with Clam Sauce 143
Oven Fried Trout 132
Oysters In a Bread Box 54
Seafood Casserole 36
Scallops St. Georges 145
Sole a la Black Friday 66
Tuna Mousse 221
Shrimp Dip 158
Ski Country Coffee 269
Skillet Potatoes 133

Smoked Wild Goose/Duck 243
Snickerdoodles 79
Soda Bread 200

SOUPS:
Avocado, Chilled 1
Broccoli, Cream of 2
Chicken Soup Mikado 102
Cream Cheese Entree 108
Creme Bordelaise 103
Fish Chowder 105
Fresh Tomato 107
Garden Room's Wild Rice 272
Grandmother's Clam Chowder 104
Ham and Pea 52
Instant Delicious Mushroom 106
Spring Borsch 53
Zucchini 109
Spaghetti Squash Primavera 136
Specials 266
Spiced Beef 28
Spicy Apple Muffins 260
Steamed Boston Brown Bread 67
Stephen Best's Best Raisin Bread 259
Strawberries Romanoff 43
Stuffed Green Peppers 118
Stuffed Pork Chops 140
Sugar Cookies 78
Summer Fruit In Wine 48

SUPPER DISHES:
Baked Pork Medallions 39
Baked Whole Salmon or Arctic Char 33
Beef Burgundy Pie 126
Beef Oyster Pie 18
Beef Stroganoff 35
Chef Bruno's Special 138
Chinese Beef and Vegetables 124
Harvester's Beef Stew 59
Lasagne 31
Moussaka 34
Nassi Goreng 131
Oven Fried Trout 132
Oysters In a Bread Box 54
Paella Espanola 30
Pierre's Chili 250
Pool Party Pie 255
Saucy Baked Beans 42
Sole a la Black Friday 66
Stuffed Pork Chops 140
Tortilla Delight 32
Triple Deck Loaf 134
Veal Cutlets Marsala 129
Veal Marengo 41
Summer Fruit In Wine 48
Swedish Almond Cream Ring 44
Sweet and Sour Chicken Balls 122
Sweet and Sour Coleslaw 11

T

Tabbouleh 241
Tea Essence 220
Telegraph House Oatcakes 188
Thelma's Unbeatable Fudge 270
Those Chocolate Macaroons 205
Tia Maria Torte 291
Tiny Pecan Tarts 218
Tomato Salad 234
Tomatoes Stuffed with Spinach 14

201

Want another "Taste"?

Please send _____ copies of A TASTE OF THE ARTS @ $12.95 each, plus $1.50 each for postage and handling. NOTE orders of five or more — 10% discount.

Make cheque or money order payable to
Edmonton Arts Cookbook Society
P.O. Box 9528
Edmonton, Alberta   T6E 5X2
Send Books To:

Prices subject to change after Dec. 31/1982

Photographs — from this book

Original photographs (16" x 20") are available at the
Middle Earth Gallery
10107 - 89 St., Edmonton
or by mailing orders to
Edmonton Arts Cookbook Society
P.O. Box 9528
Edmonton Alberta   T6E 5X2

Profits go to the Edmonton Arts Cookbook Society

Please send _____ copies of
    Picnics
    Heirlooms — top picture
    Encore — bottom picture
@ $48.00 per photo.

Please add $5.00 per order for shipping and handling.

Top picture: (from left to right
in clockwise direction)
Chilled Avocado and Consommé
Cumberland Sauce
Chen's Pockets
Wild Rice Casserole
Roast Wild Goose

Bottom picture: Candied Orange Rind
Cointreau Cheesecake

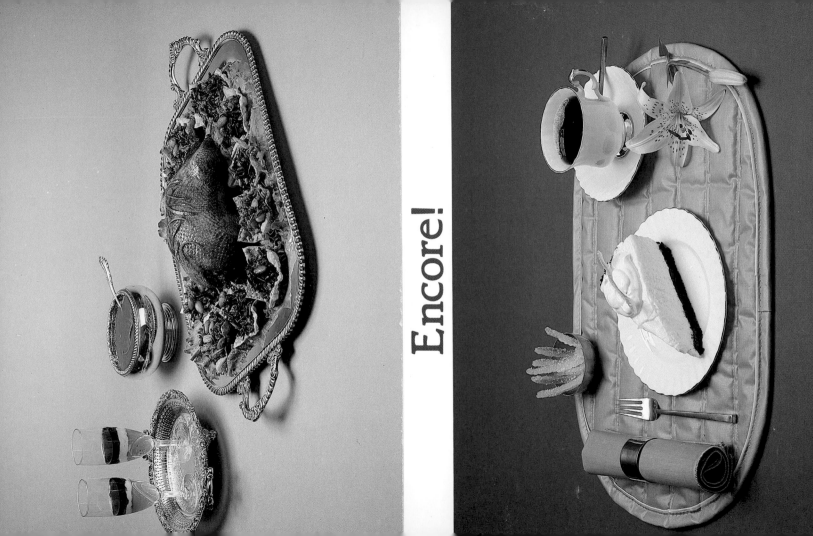

Encore!

Top picture: Avocado Crepes

Bottom picture: (from the top in
clockwise direction)
Candied Almonds
Swedish Almond Cream
with Strawberries
Daiquiri Soufflé

These recipes are for 24 or more servings. Make more for second servings.

Top picture: (in a clockwise
direction)
Oysters in a Breadbox
My Grandmother's Chutney
Calico Mustard Pickle Relish
Mustard Pickle
Old Irish Marmalade

Bottom picture: 1933 Gingersnaps
Brown Sugar Pound Cake

Heirlooms

Top picture: (clockwise from
the top)
Fresh Tomato Soup
Pasta With Prezzemolo Sauce
Papaya Salad

Bottom picture: (from left
to right)
Grapes in Brandy
Blender Pecan Torte

Midweek Gourmet

from top left in a
clockwise direction:
Oven Baked Meatballs
Lemon Chicken Wings
Mandeltorte
Cocktail Frittata
King Crab Canapes
English Muffin Wedges
Mushroom Puffs
Peppered Pecans

from top in clockwise
direction:
Smoked Duck/Goose
Sauerkraut Salad
Vegetable Pâté
Savoury French Loaf

Le Déjeuner sur l'Herbe